BEGINNER'S GUIDE

to **Adobe**®

Photoshop®

EASY LESSONS

FOR RAPID LEARNING

AND SUCCESS

Second Edition

Michelle Perkins

AMHERST MEDIA, INC. ■ BUFFALO, NY

ACKNOWLEDGMENTS

Many fine people were instrumental in the creation of this book—my great thanks go out to them all. Of special note are Kathryn and Liam Neaverth, Madeleine Lynch-Johnt, Eric Johnt, Bob Lynch, Matthew Kreib, Paul Grant, and Cody Perkins for allowing their faces to be featured herein.

Thanks also to contributing photographers Ron Nichols, Jeff Hawkins, Jeff Smith, Rick Ferro, and Paul Grant (all of whom are authors of excellent books, noted on page 126).

Barbara Lynch-Johnt provided invaluable editorial assistance and fearlessly "beta tested" all of the lessons on the Macintosh platform. Chris Boehm played PC guinea pig, testing the lessons on that system. Thanks also to photographer J.J. Allen for his helpful insights, and to readers of the first edition who offered helpful suggestions for content and presentation.

Published by:
Amherst Media, Inc.
P.O. Box 586
Buffalo, N.Y. 14226
Fax: 716-874-4508
www.AmherstMedia.com

Publisher: Craig Alesse
Assistant Editor: Barbara A. Lynch-Johnt

ISBN: 1-58428-108-1
Library of Congress Card Catalog Number: 2003103020

Printed in Korea.
10 9 8 7 6 5 4 3 2 1

TABLE OF **CONTENTS**

INTRODUCTION

▶ WHO SHOULD READ THIS BOOK

This book is designed for readers who have little or no previous experience with Adobe® Photoshop®. It teaches the basic skills needed to design attractive images for use in print, on the Internet, or in any other application you can imagine.

▶ WHAT YOU NEED TO KNOW

While you need no previous knowledge of Photoshop to use this book, it is assumed that you have the basic skills needed to use your computer. You should know how to: save and name files, print, open files, etc. Since clear, step-by-step information on installing Photoshop is provided with the software itself, you are advised to follow those instructions carefully (noting the system requirements listed on the software) and install Photoshop on your computer before beginning the lessons in this book.

▶ VERSION OF PHOTOSHOP

This book is specifically tailored for users of Photoshop 7, but much of the material will also apply to readers who wish to use earlier versions of the software. While most of Photoshop's basic tools and functions have remained the same since version 4.0, they have been upgraded, supplemented and to some degree relocated in 7.0. Of special note, earlier versions of Photoshop have a much different interface for the Text tool. Additionally, versions before 7.0 feature a separate, floating options palette.

▶ USING THIS BOOK

When you begin to use this book, note that important terms to know are defined at the beginning of each chapter. Take a minute to read these over, and refer back to them frequently. Learning the "language" of digital imaging is a skill that will make you a more efficient user of Photoshop.

To try out the techniques, you will also need one or more digital images to use as "test subjects." You will be best off using a photographic image. You can use images from a clip art collection, an image you have scanned yourself, or a shot from your digital camera.

For many sections of this book, the sample images are available as low-resolution files for download from the publisher's web site. If one or more sample images are available for a section, you'll see a computer-screen icon next to the section title. To access these, visit <www.AmherstMedia.com/downloads.htm>. Click on the title of this book and enter the password P1732. Be sure to read the important notes that accompany the images as a PDF file. (Most computers come with Adobe® Acrobat®, the software needed to open this type of file. If you do not have this program, you can download it for free at www.adobe.com.) These notes explain some settings you'll need to adjust to use these low-resolution images instead of the high-resolution versions used in the preparation of the lessons. In most cases, only the original (the "before") image file is supplied.

THE BASICS

RESOLUTION

▶ WHAT IT IS

Digital images are made up of dots called pixels. The resolution of an image tells us how close together those dots are (the dots per inch—commonly referred to as the "dpi" of an image). Images with dots that are relatively close together are said to have a "high" resolution (a high number of dots per inch). Images with dots that are relatively far apart are said to have a "low" resolution (a low number of dots per inch).

▶ WHY IT IS IMPORTANT

The resolution of an image, to a great degree, determines the apparent quality of the image. High resolution images tend to look clear and sharp—more like photographs. Low resolution images tend to look grainy, speckled, and blurry.

Does this mean you should always create the highest resolution image you can? Well, no. The more dots in an image, the more the computer has to remember and move around every time you ask it to do something with those dots. This means it will take longer for the image to open and performing operations on it will be slower. Because it is bigger, you'll also need more space on your hard drive to store a high-resolution image.

▶ WHICH RESOLUTION IS RIGHT?

So what should the resolution be? The answer is: only as high as it absolutely has to be. The precise number will be determined by what you want to do with the image.

If you want to use it on your web page, you'll select a relatively low resolution—probably 72dpi. This is all that is needed to create an acceptably sharp, clear image on a computer monitor. Anything more wouldn't make the image look any better and would increase the time it takes for the image to load onto the screen.

If you want to make an image to use in a sales pamphlet for your business, you'll need a higher

WHICH IS BIGGER?

Which is bigger, A or B? It all depends on how you look at it. Image B covers more space, but both A and B are made up of the same number of identical dots. In image A, the dots are tightly packed, giving it a high resolution. In image B, the dots are far apart, giving it a low resolution (low number of dots per inch). In the digital world, how much "space" an

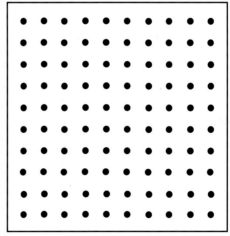
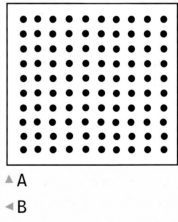

▲ A

◀ B

image covers makes very little difference. What counts is how many dots (pixels) an image is made of. This is why you'll often see digital image sizes described in terms of these dots, instead of in inches. For example, an image could be described as 500x500 (meaning it is 500 pixels tall and 500 pixels wide). As you can see in the example above, those dots could be stretched out over a lot of inches (low dpi) or packed together in a very few (high dpi). How far they are spread apart will determine the resolution of the image.

resolution—probably in the neighborhood of 300dpi. This is about the minimum required to create professionally printed materials (other than newspapers).

If you want to generate a photo-quality print on your inkjet printer, you may want to create a file as large as 700dpi.

▶ CHANGING RESOLUTION

Now, if you've already played with Photoshop, you may have noticed that it will allow you to change the resolution of an image. As nice as it would be, though, this doesn't take the place of proper planning. This is because not all pixels are created equal. Photoshop is great at moving around existing dots (making them closer together or farther apart), and is even pretty good at removing dots (reducing resolution). What Photoshop *doesn't* do well is allow you to turn 50 dots into 500 dots. If you ask Photoshop to do this, the program will have to guess where to put these dots and what they should look like. Invariably, it won't guess 100% successfully and your resulting image will appear blurry. In a pinch, you might be able to get away with having Photoshop increase the resolution by 25%—but any more than this and you'll probably not like the results.

▶ THE FINAL WORD

Don't just guess. If you're not sure what resolution you need to create the product you have in mind, find out *before* you create your file. Talk to your Internet service provider, or read the manual that came with your printer. If you'll be having someone else print your image, ask them what they recommend. There's no point in wasting your time making complicated refinements on an image that turns out to be unusable. If you'll be employing your image in multiple applications, create your scan at the largest image size (in total number of of pixels) you'll need. Then make any needed cor-

IMAGE SIZE AND RESOLUTION

How are image dimension and resolution related? There are two things to keep in mind when creating a digital image. These apply whether you are scanning a photo, using a digital camera, or making an image from scratch in Photoshop. First, ask yourself what the final dimensions of the image need to be. Do you want to make a billboard or a postage stamp? Next, determine what the final resolution of the image needs to be—72dpi? 300dpi? 1000dpi? Once you know the answers to these questions, you'll be ready to create an image (or determine if an existing image will suit your needs). All you need to do is multiply the resolution by the dimensions of the image. Here's how:

Imagine you're making a photo to put in a newsletter. The image needs to be 2" tall and 3" wide on the page, and your printer has told you that the resolution should be 300dpi. To make a file that is just the right size, multiply 2" x 300dpi (for the height) and 3" x 300 dpi (for the width). This tells you that you need an image that is 600 pixels tall and 900 pixels wide (600x900).

Later, one of the people in the photo asks if she can have a copy of this file to make an 8"x10" photo-quality print on her inkjet printer. She needs a final resolution of 700dpi. Will the same file work? Let's do the math. Your file is 600 dots tall and 900 dots wide. At 700 dots per inch, the dots would be so close together that the image would be less than an inch tall! Consequently, this file won't suit your friend's needs at all! She'll need a much larger image file—one that is 7000 dots tall (10" x 700dpi) and 5600 pixels wide (8" x 700dpi).

rections to this large file. When you've finalized the image, you can reduce its size and save multiple copies of the image for other uses.

COLOR **MODE**

▶ WHAT IT IS

If you ever took an art class (or even played around with watercolors as a kid), you probably know that combining two or more colors creates new colors. For example, combining blue paint and yellow paint makes green paint. In fact, almost all colors are actually combinations of some other colors. The exceptions (the colors you can't create by combining others) are called primary colors.

In digital imaging, the set of primary colors that are used to create all the other colors in your image is called the color mode. If your image is in the RGB mode (the most commonly used mode in Photoshop), then all of the colors in that image are made up of some combination of red (R), green (G), and blue (B). If your image is in the CMYK mode, then all of the colors in that image are made up of some combination of cyan (C), magenta (M), yellow (Y), and black (represented by the letter K). (In each of these cases, the individual color elements [the R, the G, the B; the C, the M, the Y, and the K] are called "channels." Thus, an RGB image has three channels, while a CMYK image has four channels. As you will learn, Photoshop has refined tools that allow you to make precise changes in only one channel of an image, or in all of the channels simultaneously.)

There are other color modes, too. These include grayscale (the digital imaging term for black & white) and indexed color (a special mode that can be used to streamline Internet images).

▶ WHY IT IS IMPORTANT

The way that the colors are created in an image can be important for reducing the file size of the image (perhaps to make sure it loads quickly on your web page), to improve print output, and to create special effects (such as in the duotone mode). A few common applications and their sug-

gested color modes are noted in the list below. You may find other reasons to pick one mode over another.

For this book, we will be working almost exclusively in the RGB mode. This is because it is the easiest to learn and offers the most options (most Photoshop features work in other color modes, but *all* work in RGB). Depending on how you want to use your images later, you can convert the finished versions to the desired mode. To change the color mode of an image, go to Image>Mode and select the desired color mode from the list.

COLOR MODES AND USES

RGB
- Images to be viewed on a screen (such as those used on a web page or to be e-mailed to friends)
- Images you are still working on (works in progress)
- Images you plan to print at home on your printer

CMYK
- Images that will be printed on an offset press or using other professional processes

Indexed color
- Images that need to load quickly (such as on a web page) and where perfect color reproduction is only a secondary concern

Lab color
- Occasionally used as an intermediary color mode in color correction. This is a tricky, unintuitive mode—approach with caution!

▶ WHAT IT IS

Think of the file format as the language in which the digital image is written. It tells applications, like word processing software or web browsers, that your file is a *picture* (rather than a text file, for example) and how it should handle all the data in the file to display it correctly on the screen. The file format is indicated by a tag (.tif, .jpg, etc.) added after the file name.

▶ WHY IT IS IMPORTANT

If you travel to France and try to speak Portuguese to the natives, you'll likely encounter some comprehension problems. The same thing can happen with some software applications when you ask them to understand a digital file that doesn't speak their language. Photoshop is exceptionally multilingual; it "speaks" a wide variety of file formats. Other programs aren't as well educated—many recognize only one or two file formats. If you plan to use your digital image in a program other than Photoshop, read the software's manual to determine what formats it accepts, then save your image accordingly.

Some file formats also have special features. These features may allow you to save the document in a way that facilitates later image editing on the file, or reduces the memory your computer will need to store that image. This is called compression.

▶ COMPRESSION

By reducing the amount of memory required to store an image (i.e., the file size), compression allows more images to be stored in a given space, and permits them to be transmitted over the Internet more quickly. If this sounds too good to be true, don't worry—it is (mostly). Imagine you crush a soda can. It will take up less space, but it will never look like it did to begin with. With digital compression, the same principle applies—of course, it's rather more sophisticated and your images won't look as bad as your soda can.

When an image is compressed, equations are applied to arrange the data more efficiently or to remove data that is deemed by the software to be extraneous. As a result, your image won't look as good. However, the loss in quality may not be objectionable—or it may be worth it to have an image that loads quickly on your web page.

Two file formats that offer compression are JPEG and TIF. JPEG offers "lossy" compression, meaning it removes data and significantly degrades the image. TIF offers "lossless" compression, which doesn't throw anything out, but can't compress the image as much. It's up to you to decide what you can accept, and what you can't. (Some specialized image-compression software offers small file sizes with fewer quality compromises. If you plan to use a lot of your images on the Internet, you may wish to investigate such products.)

MAJOR FILE FORMATS

TIF (.tif)
- Optional LZW "lossless" compression
- Accepted by most applications

JPEG (.jpg)
- Permits "lossy" compression
- Degree of compression determined by user
- Standard on the Internet due to small file sizes
- Not accepted by some word processing and layout applications

Photoshop (.psd)
- Permits image to be saved in most easily edited form, making later changes much easier
- Accepted by few programs other than Photoshop

WORKING WITH IMAGES

IMPORTANT TERMS

Image View—Controls that allow you to select the area of an image you want visible on your screen and how much (or little) it is enlarged.

Open—To bring an existing image file into view in Photoshop so that you can edit it.

New—To create an image file that did not originally exist.

Save—To preserve an image for future use (including further editing, viewing, and/or use in another application).

OPENING AN EXISTING IMAGE

▶ FILE > OPEN

Under the File pull-down menu at the top of your screen, click on Open. Doing so will cause a menu to appear (shown below). In this menu, you can select the image file you want to open. As noted in the captions for the image below, within this window there are several ways to refine your search for the image you want, and to get information about particular images.

▶ FILE > OPEN RECENT

Often, you won't be able to finish all the work you want to do on an image in one sitting—or you'll have a flash of inspiration about an image you were just working on. For such events, Photoshop remembers a short list of the images you have worked on most recently. To access this list, go to File>Open Recent. Under Open Recent, another submenu will appear listing the file names of the images you have recently opened in Photoshop. Simply select the correct file from this list and go to work.

With both the File>Open and File>Open Recent commands, you are opening an existing image. Therefore, the dimensions, resolution and color mode of the image will already have been set by the person who saved the image. You may wish to contrast this with opening a new image, covered on page 15.

▶ FILE > IMPORT

The File>Import command allows Macintosh users to open specialized files in the Mac-only PICT format. Both Mac and PC users can also use this command to import images from PDF (portable document format) files, a file format used to create page layouts that can be read on any computer using Adobe Acrobat. Visit the Adobe web page at <www.abode.com> for more information on this program. If you have a scanner installed on your computer, you can also access it through this command, normally by selecting TWAIN Acquire (consult the manual that came with your scanner for details).

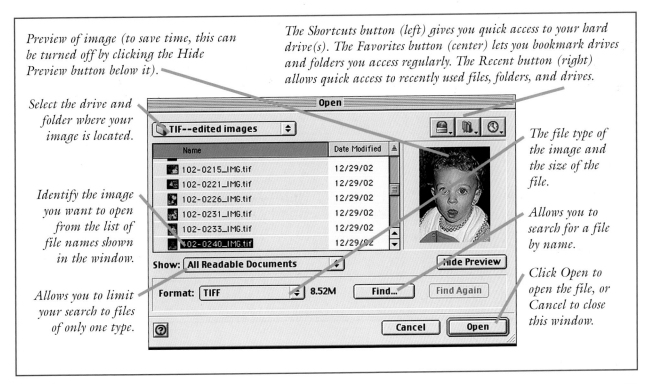

Preview of image (to save time, this can be turned off by clicking the Hide Preview button below it).

The Shortcuts button (left) gives you quick access to your hard drive(s). The Favorites button (center) lets you bookmark drives and folders you access regularly. The Recent button (right) allows quick access to recently used files, folders, and drives.

Select the drive and folder where your image is located.

Identify the image you want to open from the list of file names shown in the window.

Allows you to limit your search to files of only one type.

The file type of the image and the size of the file.

Allows you to search for a file by name.

Click Open to open the file, or Cancel to close this window.

CREATING A NEW IMAGE

▶ FILE > NEW

When you want to create a new piece of artwork (perhaps using Photoshop's painting tools, or compositing elements from several other images into one new one), you can create the digital equivalent of a blank canvas by going to File>New. Doing this will cause the dialogue box shown below to appear.

Unlike when you open an existing image, where the size and resolution of the image are already defined, when you create a new image you will need to provide some information. You will need to tell Photoshop what the dimensions of the image should be, what resolution you want, and what color mode the image should be in. You will also need to tell the program what the background color (or contents) of the new image should be. Most often, you will probably want it to be white, but you can also choose to have it transparent, or to set it to the current background color (see page 74 for more on this). (*Note:* If you select a transparent background, a white and gray checkerboard pattern will appear in the new document window. This is the standard appearance in Photoshop for a transparent background.)

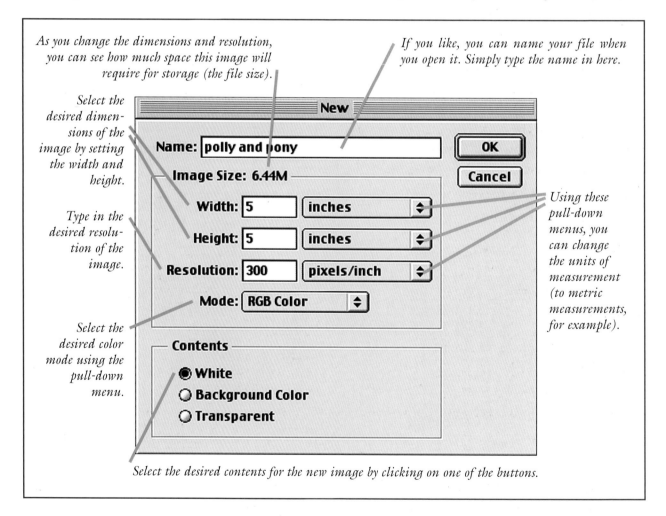

As you change the dimensions and resolution, you can see how much space this image will require for storage (the file size).

If you like, you can name your file when you open it. Simply type the name in here.

Select the desired dimensions of the image by setting the width and height.

Type in the desired resolution of the image.

Select the desired color mode using the pull-down menu.

Using these pull-down menus, you can change the units of measurement (to metric measurements, for example).

Select the desired contents for the new image by clicking on one of the buttons.

▶ WHAT IT IS

Sometimes you'll want to see the whole image, but other times you'll want to see only a part of it. There are several ways to control this. To try them out, practice with an existing image.

▶ ZOOM

In the toolbar (left) select the icon that looks like a magnifying glass. Position it over the area you want to zoom in on and click one or more times. To zoom out, hold down the Alt/Opt key (a little minus sign will appear on the magnifying glass) and click one or more times.

▶ PERCENTAGE VIEW

At the lower left corner of your document, you'll see the percentage view (below). You can type in any percentage that you like, enlarging or reducing your view of the document accordingly.

▶ SCROLLING

Once you have zoomed in, use the scroll bars at the right and bottom

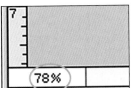

Toolbar   *Percentage view*

of the screen to move across the image and view individual areas at a higher magnification.

▶ NAVIGATOR

To view the Navigator, go to Window>Navigator. On one of the windows (called palettes), you'll see an arrangement like the ones shown below (but with your image in the center). Note the captions for details on usage.

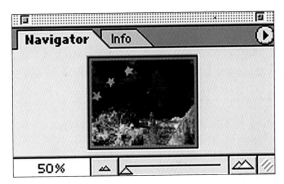

In Navigator palette, red box indicates area currently visible. Percentage at lower left indicates current view (type over it to change this). Clicking on small mountains zooms out, clicking on large mountains zooms in.

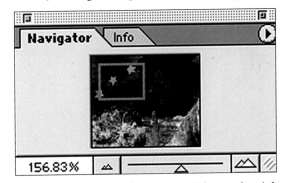

In Navigator palette, move bottom slider to the right to reduce size of area being viewed. Click and drag the red box over the area you want to see in your main window.

EDIT > UNDO

▶ WHAT IT IS

Yes, you're going to make mistakes from time to time. If you notice right away that you don't like what you just did, go to the pull-down Edit menu at the top of the screen and click Undo. This will reverse the last thing you did. Later, we'll learn how to reverse through even more steps in your progress (for those occasions where you don't notice mistakes right away, or need to backtrack more than one step)—see pages 96–97.

SAVING YOUR IMAGES

▶ SAVE

To save a new image, go to File>Save. The Save As dialogue box will then appear. In it, set the destination for the new file, enter the name of the file, and select a file format. Then hit OK. With some file formats, a second dialogue box will appear—often offering you compression options (see page 11). Set these as you like. After you have saved a file once, going to File>Save will update that file with any changes you have made (no dialogue box will appear). If you open an existing file and go to File>Save, that file will be updated with any changes you have made since opening it (or since you last saved).

▶ SAVE AS

When working on a previously-saved image, you can create a duplicate or backup by going to File>Save As. This will bring up the dialogue box shown below. From it, you can select a new destination and name for your duplicate/backup file.

▶ SAVE FOR WEB

To save an image to use on the Internet, go to File>Save for Web. From the dialogue box, you can select settings and see how long an image will take to load on a viewer's screen, as well as how it will look. You can even automatically preview the image in Microsoft® Explorer® or Netscape®.

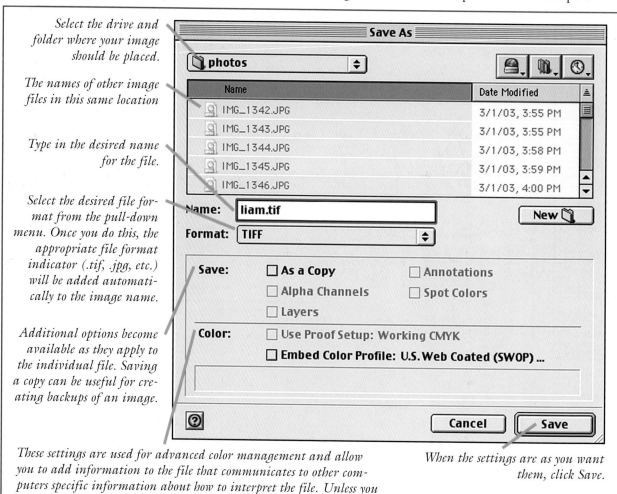

Select the drive and folder where your image should be placed.

The names of other image files in this same location

Type in the desired name for the file.

Select the desired file format from the pull-down menu. Once you do this, the appropriate file format indicator (.tif, .jpg, etc.) will be added automatically to the image name.

Additional options become available as they apply to the individual file. Saving a copy can be useful for creating backups of an image.

These settings are used for advanced color management and allow you to add information to the file that communicates to other computers specific information about how to interpret the file. Unless you have a specific need, leave these boxes unchecked. For advanced color management techniques, see the Resources list on page 122.

When the settings are as you want them, click Save.

BASIC IMAGE ENHANCEMENTS

IMPORTANT TERMS

Auto Tools—Tools that do not require the user to make any objective judgments or to adjust any settings.

Brightness—The overall lightness or darkness of the entire image.

Contrast—The difference between the lightest and darkest tones within the image.

Dialogue Box—An interactive window that, for many tools, is opened on the screen when the tool is activated. The user may then adjust the settings in this window.

AUTO LEVELS, CONTRAST, COLOR

▶ WHAT IT IS

These functions can be used to correct poor color balance or contrast. In both cases, Photoshop will reorganize the data in the image according to its own idea of what will look good. In most cases, this won't provide a complete solution, so be prepared to undo it or refine it. In some cases, it will work just fine, though, so it's worth a try!

▶ HOW TO DO IT

To use either tool, open an image in the RGB, CMYK, or grayscale mode. Go to Image>Adjustments>Auto Levels, Auto Contrast *or* Auto Color. Observe the changes. If the image looks better—great! If it looks worse, go to Edit>Undo to reverse the change. Some examples (both good and bad) are shown below and opposite.

Before: *The original image is dark, lacks contrast and is too blue. There's a lot of room for improvement!*

After: *After using the Auto Contrast tool, the overall image is improved, but it could still be better. Specifically, there is still a significant overall blue cast to the image (notice how the shadows are very blue, and the canoe is a bit more blue than neutral gray). More procedures are needed to correct the color in this image.*

Before: *The colors in this image look flat and dull. This is a common problem with scanned images.*

After: *With Auto Levels, the image is greatly improved—it doesn't need any more help.*

Before: *The contrast in this image is too low. It looks muddy and gray. It also has a bit of a yellow color cast.*

After (1): *With the Auto Levels tool, the image is greatly improved, but is still a bit yellowish in the skin tones. With a little tweaking using Photoshop's color-balancing tools (see chapter 5), this could work.*

After (2): *With Auto Contrast, the results are not as good. The contrast is good, but the color is much worse than with the Auto Levels—it's very yellow.*

After (3): *In this case, the Auto Color function seems to provide the most satisfactory result. The contrast is good and the overall color is nice. You could leave this image as is or go on to do any creative editing or retouching you like.*

VARIATIONS

▶ WHAT IT IS

This tool is one of the most intuitive in Photoshop. Using it, you can easily correct many color-balance problems in your photographs. Because it allows you to make your own judgments about how an image should look, it is much more flexible than the auto tools (Auto Contrast, Levels, and Color), yet almost as easy to use.

▶ HOW TO DO IT

To use Variations, open a color image in the RGB, CMYK, or grayscale color mode. Next, go to Image>Adjustments>Variations. Doing this will open a dialogue box like the one shown below.

Normally, you should begin with the Midtone radio button selected. This will allow you to make corrections to the tones that make up the bulk of the image. If you like, you can then select the Highlights, Shadows, or Saturation buttons and experiment with their effects on your photograph.

Near the top of the box, there is a slider that runs from Fine to Coarse. This allows you to control how great a difference you'll make with each change you apply. Start with this set at the midpoint. As you apply changes, you may find that you want to make increasingly fine adjustments. In this case, simply move the slider to the left.

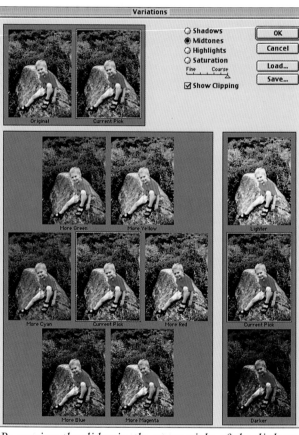

The Variations dialogue box shows numerous previews of possible image changes—More Green, More Blue, Darker, etc. By clicking on one or more of these previews, you can change your original image as you like. The effect of this change is displayed immediately in the Current Pick version of the image.

By moving the slider in the upper right of the dialogue box, you can adjust how great a difference you'll make with each change you apply. Here, the slider was set to Coarse. As you can see, the changes are much more dramatic than in the dialogue box shown on the left, where the slider was set to the midpoint.

Before: *This image is too dark and too red. Notice how the little boy's skin looks like he's been out in the sun too long. Also, the rock looks pink and the foliage in the background is a bit brown.*

After: *Using the Variations tool, blue and green were added to the image and the photograph was made a little lighter. This made a big improvement in the skin tones, rock, and foliage.*

At the top left of the dialogue box, your original image appears. This is a handy reference. If you ever decide that the changes you have made aren't helping, you can click on this image to start over.

Next to the original image, the current pick appears. The current pick also appears in the center of the color-balance samples (the cluster of seven images), and in the middle of the lighter/darker examples (the stack of three images). The current pick shows the results and is updated with every adjustment.

To begin making changes, simply click on the preview image that you think looks best (perhaps "More Green" or "Lighter"). This will automatically update the current-pick preview, so you can see the results. You can apply as many changes as

you like by clicking on one preview image after another. For some basic guidance on how to adjust the color balance in your images, consult the chart below.

IMAGE IS:	CLICK ON:
too blue	more yellow
too green	more magenta
too red	more cyan, more green
too cyan	more magenta, more red
too magenta	more green, more yellow
too yellow	more blue

BRIGHTNESS/CONTRAST

▶ WHAT IT IS

The *brightness* of an image refers to its overall lightness or darkness. The *contrast* of an image refers to the difference in brightness between the lightest and darkest tones in that image. Ideally, we can adjust these variables to produce an image with a full range of tones (from very dark to very light), where the subject is represented accurately (not too light or too dark).

Be aware, however, that both of these tools can be overused. If you make an image too bright, too dark, or too contrasty, you will lose detail in some part of that image. This may be acceptable in some cases, but is usually not desirable. Therefore, use these tools carefully.

▶ HOW TO DO IT

To use the Brightness/Contrast tool, go to Image>Adjustments>Brightness/Contrast. This will open a dialogue box like the one shown below. Make sure the Preview box is checked, so that you will be able to see an immediate preview

of the changes as you make adjustments. Then, begin to move the sliders.

In most cases, you'll want to increase the contrast (move the bottom slider to the right of center). Keep an eye on the darkest and lightest areas of your image as you do so. If you adjust the contrast so that it is very high, you'll see that these areas will start to lose detail (becoming pure white or pure black). If you want to create a natural-looking image, this is something you generally want to avoid.

You can use your own judgment when adjusting the brightness of the image. Depending on the subject matter, the style of the image, and the look you are going for, the adjustments you make may vary widely from image to image.

Some examples (both good and bad) of the adjustment of brightness/contrast are shown on the facing page.

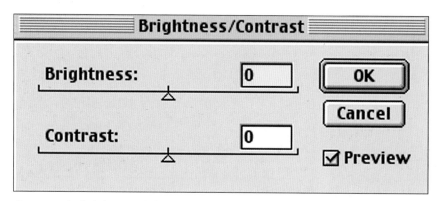

Increase the brightness of the image by moving the top slider to the right of center. Increase the contrast of the image by moving the bottom slider to the right of center. Leaving the Preview box checked will allow you to immediately preview the changes being made as you move each slider.

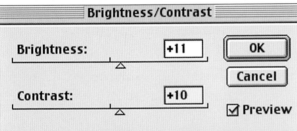

Top left: *Original color photograph.*

Left: *Adjustments were made in the Brightness/Contrast dialogue box to brighten the image and boost its contrast.*

Top right: *Corrected color image—a big improvement!*

Original color photograph. This image is too dark and lacks contrast.

After correcting the image using the Brightness/Contrast tool, there's some improvement. However, there is still a blue-green color cast. Techniques for removing color casts are presented on pages 40–48.

INVERT

▶ WHAT IT IS

Inverting an image creates a negative. This means that all of the tones are changed to their opposites.

▶ HOW TO DO IT

Begin with an image in the RGB or grayscale mode. Go to Image>Adjustments>Invert. The colors will change as follows:

Original color image.

Inverted image.

COLOR:	CHANGES TO:
blue	yellow
green	magenta
red	cyan
cyan	red
magenta	green
yellow	blue
black	white
white	black

Original black & white image.

Inverted image.

POSTERIZE

▶ WHAT IT IS

Posterizing an image allows you to alter the image to contain a set number of tones. Traditionally, this tool was used to turn a grayscale image into one that contained only pure black and white. With Photoshop, you can posterize color images, too, and select the number of tones to include.

▶ HOW TO DO IT

Go to Image>Adjustments>Posterize. Select a number of tones. (Leave the Preview box checked so that you can see the results.) You can adjust the number of tones as many times as you want until you achieve an effect you like.

Original black & white image.

Posterized image with two levels.

Original color image.

Posterized image with two levels.

USING FILTERS

IMPORTANT TERMS

Filter—A digital tool used to apply a specialized effect to an image.

Fade—Reduces the apparent impact of the filter on the image.

ABOUT FILTERS

▶ WHAT THEY ARE

A filter is a specialized piece of software that runs within Photoshop and is used to apply a specific effect to an image. Many filters are packaged with Photoshop itself, and other filters (from Adobe® and other companies) are also available to meet specialized needs. In this book, we'll stick to the ones that are packaged with Photoshop.

▶ HOW TO USE THEM

To use any filter, go to the filter menu. Pulling this down will reveal several submenus that contain groups of filters. Select any filter to apply it. Some will apply immediately, some will open a dialogue box and ask you to customize the settings for the effect you want. On pages 27–38, we will look at samples of filters and how to use them.

FILTERS AND COLOR MODE

▶ WHY IT'S IMPORTANT

Not all filters are available for use by images in all color modes. To make all of the filters available, you should work with an image in the RGB mode.

▶ HOW TO DO IT

To check the color mode of your image, go to Image>Mode and note which mode is checked in the list. If the image is not in the RGB mode, change it by selecting RGB Color from this same list.

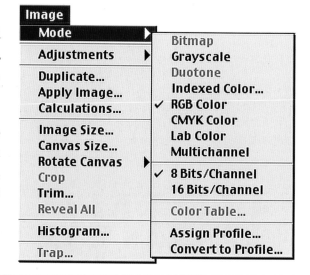

FADE

▶ WHAT IT IS

Once you have applied a filter to your image, you may decide that the effect is stronger than you would like. Using the fade command will allow you to reduce the effect of the filter.

▶ HOW TO DO IT

The fade command can only be used *immediately* after the application of the filter. To access it, go to Edit>Fade (*Name of Filter*). Use the slider to reduce the effect of the filter. Make sure the Preview box is checked so you can evaluate the changes you are making as you make them. You

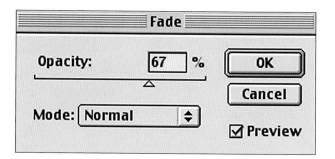

can also change something called the Mode from this window. This will be discussed in detail on page 89, but you can experiment with it now, if you like.

▶ WHAT IT IS

The filters in this group are designed to imitate the effects of traditional artistic media. For most, you will have the chance to enter settings in a dialogue box. A few examples are shown below. Experiment with these filters and their settings as much as you like—you can always use the Edit>Undo command to reverse the effect if you don't like it.

The filters included in this category are: Colored Pencil, Cutout, Dry Brush, Film Grain, Fresco, Neon Glow, Paint Daubs, Palette Knife, Plastic Wrap, Poster Edges, Rough Pastels, Smudge Stick, Sponge, Underpainting, and Watercolor. Each filter has slightly different controls and effects. The best way to learn to use them is to open an image and begin experimenting.

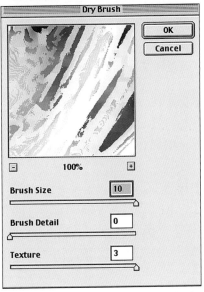
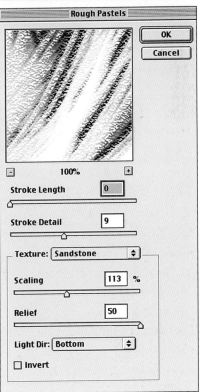

Above: *Original color photograph.*

Center top: *Photo with Dry Brush filter applied.*

Center bottom: *The dialogue box for the Dry Brush filter allows you to select the brush size, the amount of detail produced by the brush, and the amount of texture depicted. At the top, a Preview box shows you the effect of your changes. Hit OK to apply the filter to your image.*

Right top: *Photo with Rough Pastels filter applied.*

Right bottom: *The dialogue box for the Rough Pastels filter allows you to select the stroke length and detail, the medium the brush is applied to (canvas, brick, etc.), and the degree of texture of the background. You can also control the direction from which light seems to fall on the texture.*

BLUR

▶ WHAT IT IS

The filters under the Blur header allow you to reduce sharpness in an image. This can be useful for creating a "soft focus" effect that hides details, or for adding special effects (like a motion blur).

The filters included in this category are: Blur, Blur More, Gaussian Blur, Motion Blur, Radial Blur, and Smart Blur. Of these, Gaussian Blur is the most flexible and intuitive tool, allowing you to create a smooth, all-over blur. The Blur and Blur More filters also create an all-over blur, but do not allow you to control the degree of blurring. The Radial and Motion Blur filters are useful for creating special effects. Smart Blur softens areas of similar tone while trying to maintain sharp edges.

Above: *Original color photograph.*

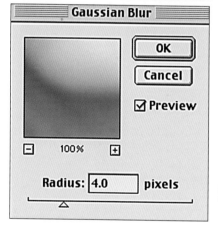

Top: *Photo with Gaussian Blur filter applied.*

Bottom: *The dialogue box for the Gaussian Blur filter. Increase the blur radius (measured in pixels) by moving the slider to the right.*

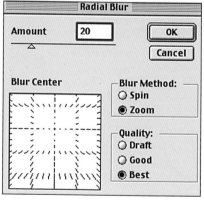

Top: *Photo with Radial Blur filter applied.*

Bottom: *The dialogue box for the Radial Blur filter. After selecting the amount of blur, Zoom was selected as the blur method and the Quality was set to Best. Using the mouse to click and drag, the Blur Center was moved over the subject's face.*

BRUSH STROKES

▶ WHAT IT IS

The filters in the brush stroke group can be used to add the look of natural brush strokes to an image. The filters included in this category are: Accented Edges, Angled Strokes, Crosshatch, Dark Strokes, Ink Outlines, Spatter, Sprayed Strokes, and Sumi-e.

▶ HOW TO DO IT

When you select the filter you want to apply, a dialogue box will appear. In this box, you will be able to set parameters for the length of the brush strokes and their pressure (selections vary slightly from filter to filter). Use the preview window to adjust and evaluate the settings.

Original color photograph.

Accented Edges filter applied.

Crosshatch filter applied.

Spatter filter applied.

Sprayed Strokes filter applied.

Sumi-e filter applied.

DISTORT

▶ WHAT IT IS

The filters in the distort group add waves and other distortion effects to images.

▶ ABOUT THE FILTERS

The filters in this group are quite varied in their effects. The most interesting (and easy to use) of these are:

- **Diffuse Glow**—Applies a misty glow to your image.
- **Glass**—Adds shiny highlights and texture to your image. You can select from the look of frosted glass, glass blocks, etc.

- **Ocean Ripple, Ripple, Wave, Zigzag**— Enhance your image with wave effects (each adjusted using slightly different sets of controls). The Zigzag filter offers a nice pond-ripple setting, for example. Applied to extremes, all create interesting abstracts.
- **Pinch**—Makes the center of the image appear to be pinched in.
- **Spherize**—Makes the center of the image appear to bulge out.
- **Polar Coordinates, Twirl**—Twists your image either from the center or around an edge point.

Original color photograph.

Diffuse Glow filter applied.

Pinch filter applied.

Glass filter (set to glass blocks) applied.

Wave filter applied.

Zigzag filter (set to pond ripples) applied.

▶ WHAT IT IS

The filters in this group can be used to add noise (a speckled look somewhat like a grainy photograph), as well as to correct dust and scratches and despeckle images.

While the Noise filter is good for adding the look of grain to an image (see below), the Despeckle and Dust & Scratches filters are less than perfect. This is because they rely on the computer to make decisions about what is dust (or a scratch or a speck), and usually the computer won't make the same decisions you would. The result is typically that, along with the dust or scratches, you will lose some of the *desirable* detail in the image. On pages 78–79, you'll learn a better, more precise way to remove small imperfections.

Also included in this group is something called the Median filter. This is a primitive version of the Dust & Scratches filter (and an artifact from very early versions of Photoshop). It selects the average (median) color based on the radial distance you select from the dialogue box.

Original color photograph.

Noise filter applied (6%).

Dust & Scratches filter applied (radius 3 pixels, threshold 0).

Median filter applied (radius 4 pixels).

PIXELATE

The pixelate filters create a number of stylized effects. Essentially, these filters function by breaking the image into clumps—circles, squares and other patterns. When using these filters, select a relatively low setting in the dialogue box, or your image will become unrecognizable.

The Color Halftone and Mezzotint filters replicate the look of traditional printing techniques. The Mosaic, Fragment, Facet, and Crystallize filters break the image up into cells (geometric areas of a single color) of varying shapes. The size of the cell is set in the dialogue box.

The Pointillize filter is probably the most useful one in this set, since it replicates the look of a traditional painting technique. In the style of a subgroup of the French Impressionists (called Pointillists), this filter renders the image as groups of tiny dots of color. As long as you keep the cell size small, your eye will blend these dots together into a stylized but unified image.

Original color photograph.

Color Halftone filter applied (default).

Crystallize filter applied (cell size 15).

Mezzotint filter applied (short strokes).

Mosaic filter applied (10 squares).

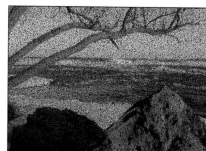
Pointillize filter applied (cell size 6).

▶ WHAT IT IS

The render filters produce special 3-D shapes, clouds, refraction patterns, and simulated light effects. These are mathematically intensive filters and may take a while to apply to your image.

▶ ABOUT THE FILTERS

- **3D Transform**—Allows you to "wrap" your picture over a virtual cylinder, cube, or sphere (in the dialogue box, select the appropriate shape, then click and drag over the image preview). You can view your image from different perspectives using the pan and tilt features.
- **Clouds**—Creates clouds based on the foreground and background colors. The on-screen image doesn't affect how they look.
- **Difference Clouds**—Similar to the Clouds filter, but incorporates data from the image on the screen. (Try applying this filter ten or more times sequentially to create a pattern that looks somewhat like marble.)
- **Lens Flare**—Simulates the washed out effect and geometric shapes created when bright light strikes a camera lens. Specify the center of the flare by clicking inside the image preview or dragging the crosshairs.
- **Lighting Effects**—Allows you to apply a variety of light sources (from flashlights to spotlights) to your image. This is a slightly complicated filter to use. Begin by selecting a style (from the top pull-down menu). Then adjust the direction by clicking and dragging to

Original photograph.

Difference Clouds filter applied.

Lens Flare filter applied.

Lighting Effects filter applied.

rotate the light in the preview of your image. Other settings in the dialogue box fine-tune the effect—the best way to learn to use these is simply to experiment!

- **Texture Fill**—Fills a selection with all or part of a grayscale file. To add texture, you open the grayscale document you want to use as the texture fill.

SHARPENING

▶ WHAT IT IS

The sharpening filters allow you to improve the sharpness of your images. They are only useful for correcting minor problems, however. If your image looks blurry to the naked eye, you're probably out of luck. If it looks pretty much okay to the naked eye, but a little fuzziness is apparent when you really get critical (or look at it with a magnifying glass), sharpening may do the trick. Additionally, almost every scan of an image (from a print, slide, etc.) requires at least a little sharpening to make it look as crisp as the original.

▶ HOW TO DO IT

To sharpen an image, go to Filter>Sharpen and select the tool you want to use. As noted below, some filters run automatically, while others require you to adjust their settings.

▶ SHARPEN

The Sharpen filter automatically applies itself to every pixel in the image (or in a selected area [see pages 52–58 for information on making selections]). It works by enhancing the contrast between adjoining pixels, creating the appearance of sharper focus.

▶ SHARPEN EDGES

This filter works pretty much like the Sharpen filter, except that it seeks out the edges of objects and enhances those areas to create the illusion of increased sharpness. Photoshop identifies edges by looking for differences in color and contrast between adjacent pixels.

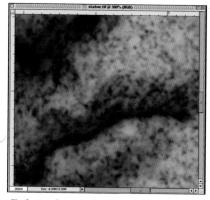
Enlarged section of original photo.

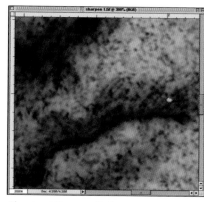
Sharpen filter applied.

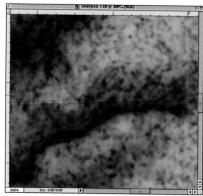
Sharpen Edges filter applied.

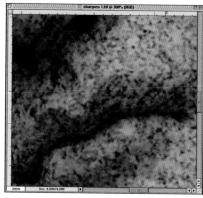
Sharpen More filter applied.

▶ SHARPEN MORE

Like the Sharpen filter, the Sharpen More filter affects every pixel. As the name implies, it does so more strongly than the Sharpen filter.

HINTS AND TIPS

All of the sharpening filters can be run multiple times sequentially, and/or in combination with each other. You'll need to tailor your approach to each image—and be prepared to experiment with a few different settings and methods.

Oversharpening can occur easily, actually degrading image quality, rather than enhancing it. Watch out for glowing edges and speckled areas on your image; these can be indicators that you've sharpened it too much.

▶ UNSHARP MASK

This is the most powerful sharpening tool in Photoshop. As you become comfortable using it, you'll probably find you want to employ it on nearly every image you deal with. Follow the steps below to use the filter, but be prepared for some experimentation—every image is unique and sharpening decisions are highly subjective.

To begin, go to Filter>Sharpen>Unsharp Mask. This will bring up the dialogue box shown below (be sure to activate the preview). In this box, you can adjust the amount of sharpening (how much sharpening occurs), the radius (how far from each pixel the effect is applied) and the threshold (how similar in value the pixels must be to be sharpened. To get started, try setting the amount to 150%, the radius to 1–2 pixels and the threshold to 10 levels. Watch the preview and fine-tune these settings until you like the results.

Watch out for oversharpening (example below). If you're not sure you've sharpened an image correctly, go to Edit>Undo and compare the new version to the original. If the new one *was* better, use Edit>Redo to return to it.

Many people find that the most natural-looking results are achieved by setting the filter for very light sharpening, then applying it several times.

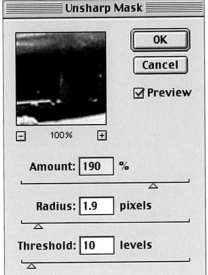
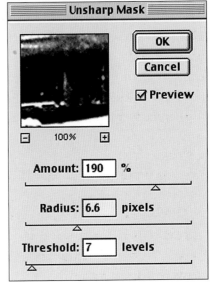

Above: *Original photo.*
Center: *Photo with good sharpening.*
Right: *Photo with too much sharpening.*

SKETCH

▶ WHAT IT IS

The sketch filters imitate the look of the various media used in sketching, as well as some other paper-based artistic processes. These filters include: Bas Relief, Chalk and Charcoal, Charcoal, Chrome, Conté Crayon, Graphic Pen, Halftone Paper, Note Paper, Photocopy, Plaster, Reticulation, Stamp, Torn Edges, and Water Paper. The effect of each filter is controlled through a dia-logue box that opens when you select the filter. The best way to learn about these filters and the best settings for them is simply to experiment!

▶ HOW TO DO IT

For best results, use a black & white image. This must be in either the grayscale or RGB mode, as these filters cannot be used on images in the CMYK color mode.

Original black & white photograph.

Bas Relief filter applied.

Charcoal filter applied.

Photocopy filter applied.

Stamp filter applied.

Water Paper filter applied.

Original color image. Sometimes, photographs taken under blue skies look too blue and lack the warmth our eyes saw in the scene.

Final image. Adjusting the color balance of the photograph can restore that warmth.

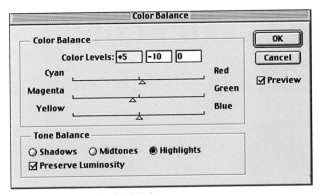

Adjustment to the highlights.

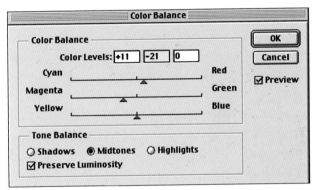

Adjustment to the midtones.

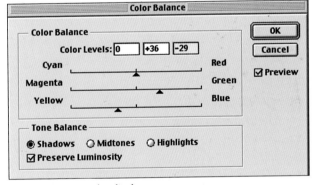

Adjustment to the shadows.

Once you feel comfortable adjusting the Color Balance settings for the midtones, you can move on to experiment with adjusting the balance in the highlights (brighter areas) and shadows (darker areas). In the Tone Balance box, simply click on the tonal range you want to adjust.

You can adjust all of these ranges in a single image by switching back and forth between the tonal ranges. As you move between the ranges, Photoshop will save your settings in each one—meaning you can adjust the highlights, then the midtones, then go back to the highlights, etc. When your image looks the way you want it to, hit OK to apply your changes.

▶ ANOTHER EXAMPLE

The Color Balance tool can be very useful for removing the color casts caused by lighting conditions. Under incandescent lighting (household lights), colors can look too yellow. Under fluorescent lights, colors can look too green. Even under open skies, colors can sometimes look too blue. The Color Balance tool is ideal for adjusting these.

HUE/SATURATION

▶ WHAT IT IS

The Hue/Saturation tool (Image>Adjustments> Hue/Saturation) has two interesting functions. The first function allows you to select a range of colors from an image (say, all the red tones or all the green tones) and adjust them without changing any of the other tones in the image. With the Colorize feature activated, the Hue/Saturation tool allows you to render an image in a monotone color of your choice—excellent for creating the look of a classic sepia-toned image or a more contemporary dyed image.

▶ MODIFY A SELECTED COLOR

This function is very useful for correcting images where there is a discrete area of a unique color that needs to be changed. For example, in the photo to the right, the girl's blue shirt is basically the only blue tone in the image.

To adjust its color, the Hue/Saturation tool was used. In the dialogue box, Blues was selected in the pull-down Edit menu. Then, the Hue slider was moved until the shirt was the desired color (see the top two images on the facing page). This works well because her shirt is basically the only blue element in the photo. If, for example, there had been blue flowers in the background, these would have changed color with the shirt—perhaps making the effect less desirable.

▶ COLORIZE AN IMAGE

When you activate the Colorize box in the Hue/ Saturation dialogue box, you'll notice an immediate change. The photo will become monotone—like a black & white image but with some color other than black. You can select that color by moving the Hue slider to the left or right. At the bottom of the facing page, you'll see two examples. In the first one (left), the Hue slider was moved to the right to create the look of a dyed image. In the

Original color photograph (courtesy of Ron Nichols).

second (right), the slider was moved to the left to create the look of a sepia-toned photograph.

▶ SATURATION AND LIGHTNESS

You'll notice two additional sliders located below the Hue slider. Once a hue is selected using the top slider, the Saturation slider allows you to adjust the intensity of that color. The best way to see this at work is to give it a try. Select a color with the Hue slider, then move the Saturation slider to the left to reduce saturation and to the right to increase saturation. When modifying selected colors, you'll probably use this adjustment infrequently. When using the Colorize feature (as seen at the bottom of the facing page), it is often desirable to slightly reduce the saturation of the new color in the image.

The Lightness slider can be used to adjust the overall lightness or darkness of an image. This control will adjust the brightness/darkness universally throughout the image—in the shadows, midtones and highlights. To lighten, move the slider to the right. To darken, move it to the left.

After selecting Blues from the Edit menu, the Hue slider was moved to the right. This changed the girl's blue shirt to lavender.

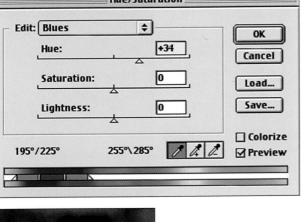

After selecting Blues from the Edit menu, the Hue slider was moved to the left. This changed the girl's blue shirt to green.

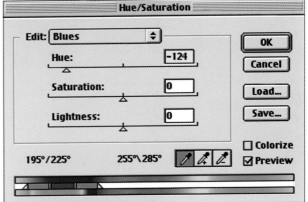

With the Colorize function selected, a purple hue was selected and the saturation was dropped. This created the look of a dyed image.

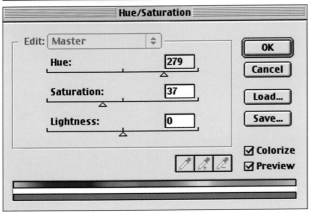

With the Colorize function selected, a peach-brown hue was selected and the saturation was dropped. This created the look of a sepia-toned image.

SELECTIVE COLOR

▶ WHAT IT IS

The Selective Color (Image>Adjustments>Selective Color) tool allows you to make corrections to the color balance of individual color channels in an image. For example, if you notice that all the red tones in an image look too pink or too orange,

Original color image.

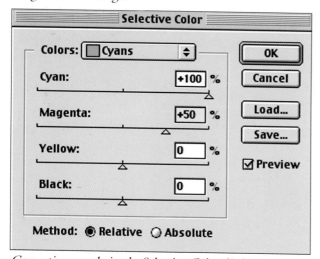
Corrections made in the Selective Color dialogue box.

Adjusted color image.

you can select the red channel and adjust these red tones without affecting the other colors in the image.

▶ HOW TO DO IT

When you go to Image>Adjustments>Selective Color, a dialogue box will appear. At the top of this box is a pull-down menu of colors. Pull down on this list and select the color that most closely describes the color range you want to alter. Make sure the Preview box is also checked so you can see the effect your changes have as you make them.

Next, select the Relative setting at the bottom of the box. This will limit the adjustments to areas where the selected color is present. (If you select Absolute, you can add color to all the tones in the image, even if the selected color component is not present in them.) Then, adjust the individual color sliders to shift the selected color as you desire. In the example to the left, cyan was selected (the primary color in the sky). The cyan was increased and additional magenta was added to create a richer tone in the sky.

Sometimes, the color you want to change may fall between two categories (for instance, orange or purple). In these cases, you may need to adjust two (or more) colors to make the correction. For example, to adjust orange tones, try working with the red and yellow channels. For purple, try adjusting the blue and red (or blue and magenta) channels. To do this, simply select the first color to change and make your adjustments. Then, return to the Colors pull-down menu and select another color to adjust.

When your corrections are complete, hit OK to apply them.

TOOLS FOR MAKING SELECTIONS

IMPORTANT TERMS

Active Selection—An area of an image isolated using one of the selection tools and marked off by a dotted black & white line.

Cropping—Removing extraneous areas from the edges of a photograph.

Deactivate Selection—To eliminate an active selection by clicking anywhere on the image.

Toolbar—Normally located at the upper-left corner of the screen, the toolbar allows users to choose brushes, selection devices, and other tools used in creating images.

Tool Options—Settings that are determined by the user and allow tools to be customized to perform in a specialized way. Each tool has its own set of options (though some overlap). Options are displayed and accessed via the options palette at the top of the screen.

TOOLBAR **OVERVIEW**

▶ WHAT IT IS

As you will have noticed, so far we have only used functions of Photoshop that are accessed using the pull-down menus at the top of the screen. However, some of the most useful tools are found in the toolbar (right). If the toolbar is not visible on your screen, go to Window>Tools.

As you read through the notes on the toolbar shown to the right, you'll see that the tools are loosely grouped by function (painting tools, selection tools, etc.) and that many have multiple functions. To identify tools with multiple functions, look for the small black triangle at the lower right corner of the tool icon. This indicates that you can click and hold on this tool to reveal additional options.

▶ HOW TO USE IT

To select a tool, simply click on it. The icon you click on will become dark gray, indicating that it is the currently selected tool.

In the following sections, we will explore the features and functions of these tools. You may wish to refer back to this diagram as you complete these lessons.

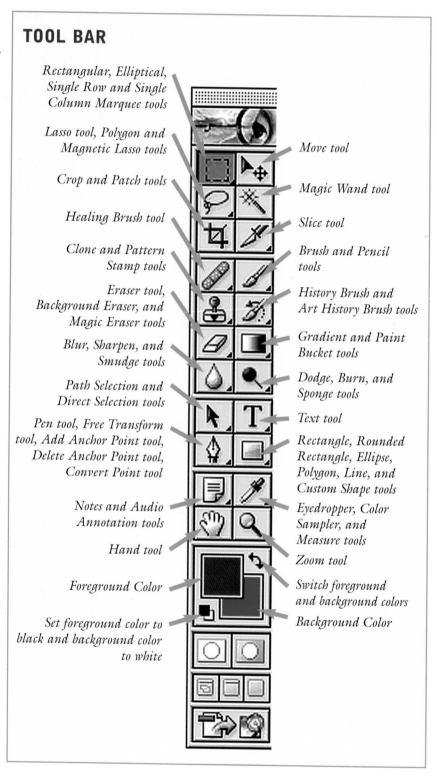

TOOL BAR

Rectangular, Elliptical, Single Row and Single Column Marquee tools

Lasso tool, Polygon and Magnetic Lasso tools

Crop and Patch tools

Healing Brush tool

Clone and Pattern Stamp tools

Eraser tool, Background Eraser, and Magic Eraser tools

Blur, Sharpen, and Smudge tools

Path Selection and Direct Selection tools

Pen tool, Free Transform tool, Add Anchor Point tool, Delete Anchor Point tool, Convert Point tool

Notes and Audio Annotation tools

Hand tool

Foreground Color

Set foreground color to black and background color to white

Move tool

Magic Wand tool

Slice tool

Brush and Pencil tools

History Brush and Art History Brush tools

Gradient and Paint Bucket tools

Dodge, Burn, and Sponge tools

Text tool

Rectangle, Rounded Rectangle, Ellipse, Polygon, Line, and Custom Shape tools

Eyedropper, Color Sampler, and Measure tools

Zoom tool

Switch foreground and background colors

Background Color

TOOL OPTIONS

▶ WHAT IT IS

Just as an artist can select the precise paintbrush she needs to create the effect she wants, the tools in Photoshop are equipped with an options palette that allows them to be customized for each task. This palette looks a little different than other palettes, as it is permanently placed just under the pull-down menus at the top of the screen.

As you select tools on the toolbar, keep an eye on this area. You'll notice that it changes, offering a different set of options for each tool you select. You'll also see the icon for the selected tool repeated at the left of the palette (as shown below).

As we begin to use these tools individually, you will learn how to select the right options for your application and how the versatility of each tool improves your ability to work with images.

▶ RESET TOOLS

When a tool doesn't work the way it seems it ought to, it's often because you've changed one

(or more) of its options. If this happens, try resetting the tool. To do this, in the options palette, click on the down arrow to the right of the tool icon (at the extreme left edge of the palette) to open the tool presets window. Click on the arrow at the top right of this palette and select Reset Tool from the pull-down menu.

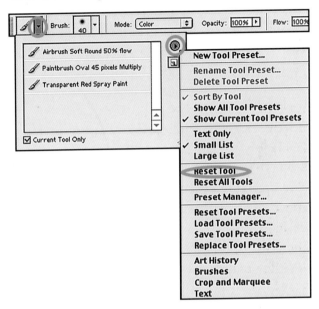

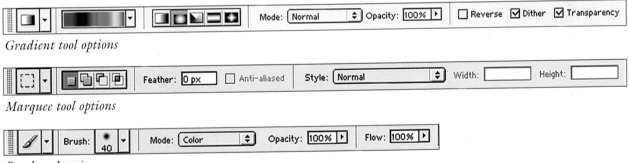

Gradient tool options

Marquee tool options

Brush tool options

SELECTIONS

▶ WHAT IT IS

The selection tools are designed to allow you to isolate parts of an image (or, in the case of the Crop tool, to eliminate parts of the image).

So far, all of the image changes we've learned about have been applied to the entire image. Frequently, however, you'll want to make changes to only one area. The selection tools allow you to isolate the area that needs work and apply your changes to that area alone.

▶ HOW TO DO IT

Selected areas are indicated by a flashing dotted black & white line (often called "marching ants") around the area. Making this line fall exactly where you want it to around irregularly shaped subjects is the key to making accurate selections. In fact, developing accurate selection techniques is one of the most challenging skills new Photoshop users need to acquire. While the tools themselves are quite easy to learn to use, some practice will be required to develop your instincts about which tool is best for each situation. Often, a combination of tools is required. Once these techniques are mastered, however, the sky is the limit!

Below, you will find just one example of how selections can be used to enhance your images. In this case, it was used to create a vignette (a darkened area) around the subject.

> **WARNING!**
> Once you have made a selection using the techniques that follow, **DO NOT** click anywhere else on your image with a selection tool. Doing so will deactivate (eliminate) your selection. (On page 66, you will learn how to save a selection. On pages 96–97 you will learn how to use the history palette to reactivate a selection.)

Original photograph (courtesy of Ron Nichols).

The outer parts of the photo are selected. This means that only these areas (and not the central area with the subject) will be affected by the changes made.

The selected areas are darkened, creating a vignette that helps focus the viewer's eye on the subject.

▶ WHAT IT IS

The Crop tool is used to remove extraneous areas from the edges of a photograph. Although it is grouped with the selection tools in the toolbar (see page 50), it is not a selection tool in the same sense as the others in this group. For this reason, when the term "selection tool" is used on the following pages, this reference does *not* include the Crop tool. Using it, however, is a good introduction to making selections.

▶ HOW TO DO IT

To crop an image, select the Crop tool from the toolbar. Click and drag over the area of your image that you want to keep, then release your mouse button. You don't have to be incredibly precise. At each corner of the crop indicator (the dotted line) you will see small boxes. These are handles that you can click and drag to reshape or reposition the box. (As you get near the edges of the photo, these handles tend to "stick" to the edges. To prevent this, click on the handle you want to drag, then click and hold down the Control key.) When the cropped area looks right, hit Enter to apply the change.

▶ STRAIGHTENING CROOKED IMAGES

The Crop tool can also be used to straighten a crooked image. Simply click and drag over the image with the Crop tool, then position your mouse over one of the corner handles until the cursor's arrow icon turns into a bent-arrow icon. Once you see this, click and rotate the crop indicator as needed. An example of this (and cropping to remove extraneous material) is shown to the right.

▶ CROPPING TOOL OPTIONS

In the options palette at the top of the screen are two useful adjustments. When you first select the Crop tool, you have the option to select a target size (the final size of the cropped image). This is helpful if, for instance, you specifically want to create a 3"x5" print to frame. Simply enter the desired height, width, and resolution needed and crop as usual. The Crop tool will constrain itself to the desired proportions. Once you have selected the area to be cropped, the area to be cropped *out* (removed) can also be grayed out in the preview so you can best evaluate the results. Simply select the Shield Cropped Area option in the options palette and set the opacity as you like.

Left: *Original photograph.*

Below left: *The area of the photograph containing the subject is selected with the cropping tool.*

Below: *The final cropped image, with most of the surrounding, extraneous background removed from the frame.*

CROPPING AND RESOLUTION

Cropping reduces your total image size (the number of pixels), a factor that must be taken into account. You may wish to scan your image at a higher resolution to compensate (see pages 8–9).

MARQUEE

▶ WHAT IT IS

The Marquee tool (see page 50) is used to make rectangular, square, circular, or elliptical selections. In the toolbar, click and hold on the Marquee tool icon to reveal the pull-down menu seen below. You can then select the tool you need.

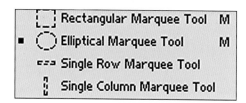

▶ HOW TO DO IT

Decide whether the area you want to select is square/rectangular or round/elliptical and select the appropriate tool. Then, click and drag over the area of the image you want to select. You'll probably need to practice this a few times to get the hang of it and to end up with the selection exactly where you want it to be. This is especially true with the Elliptical Marquee tool, which can be quite tricky to master. (If you prefer, instead of drawing the selected shape from its edge, you can draw from the center by holding down the Alt/Opt key before you click and drag.)

▶ PERFECT SQUARES, PERFECT CIRCLES

When you select the Marquee tool, then click and drag over your image, you do so "freehand." Often, however, you may want to select a perfectly square or perfectly round area. To do this, simply select the Marquee tool (either rectangular or elliptical), press and hold the Shift key, then click and drag over your image. This is a very helpful option, since very few people possess the coordination or sense of perspective required to draw a perfect geometric square or circle.

▶ MARQUEE OPTIONS

To make a selection of a fixed size or aspect ratio (proportion of height to width), make the appropriate selection from the Style menu in the options palette. Then, enter the measurements or values you desire in the boxes next to this menu. Because they are critical and essentially identical for each tool, the other options for the Marquee, Lasso, and Magic Wand tools are discussed in chapter 7.

Right: *Original color photograph.*

Below: *Using the Marquee tool, squares and rectangles of various sizes and shapes were selected throughout the frame. After making each individual selection, a filter from the artistic group was applied to the area. Combining overlapping selections with a filter effect created this look.*

TIPS

• To reposition a selection, before releasing the mouse button, press amd hold the Shift key, then drag the selection into place. If you have already released the mouse button, select the Marquee tool, then click and hold within the selected area. While holding the button down, drag the selection into place.

• To deactivate a selection, click outside the selection with the Marquee tool.

Original color photograph.

▶ WHAT IT IS

The Lasso tool is used to make irregular selections. It has three variations: Lasso, Polygonal Lasso, and Magnetic Lasso. Click and hold on the Lasso tool in the toolbar (see page 50) to reveal the menu seen below. Then, select the tool you need.

▶ USING THE LASSO

The Lasso tool is used to draw around an area using a continuous line. This line can be made up of any combination of straight and curved areas. To use it, select the Lasso tool, click on one edge of the area to be selected, then drag your cursor around the perimeter of the area to be selected.

▶ USING THE POLYGONAL LASSO

The Polygonal Lasso tool allows you to create geometric selections. To use this tool, select it, then click on one of the corners of the area to be selected. Release the mouse button, move the cursor to the next corner and click the mouse. Repeat until the entire shape is selected.

▶ USING THE MAGNETIC LASSO

The Magnetic Lasso tool is similar to the freehand Lasso, but it tries to help you make more accurate selections by automatically "sticking" to lines in the image. To use it, select the Magnetic Lasso tool, click on one edge of the area to be selected, then move your cursor around the perimeter of the area to be selected. When you finish, hit Enter. Specialized settings in the options palette are used to control what the Lasso "sticks" to. Lasso width controls how important the detected edge is versus the actual path of your mouse. Frequency controls how smooth you are able to make curves.

The Lasso tool was used to carefully select the pigs. With the selection still active, the Hue/Saturation tool (Image>Adjustments>Hue/Saturation was used). It was set to colorize to turn the pigs blue.

TIPS FOR THE LASSO TOOL

- You must end the selection where you began it (make a closed shape).
- To draw a perfectly straight horizontal or vertical line, press and hold the Shift key while you are tracing the edge of your selection.

Edge Contrast tells Photoshop how to decide what's a line and what's not. Be prepared! This takes a good deal of practice to master.

MAGIC WAND

▶ WHAT IT IS

The Magic Wand is a selection tool that is used to select areas based on their color. It is very useful when you need to select an irregularly shaped area with little or no tonal variations (like all the blue areas in a sky with scattered white clouds).

▶ HOW TO DO IT

Select the Magic Wand from the toolbar (see page 50). Identify the area to be selected. Click on one point in that area. The Magic Wand will automatically select that point and all other contiguous points of the same color.

▶ MAGIC WAND TOOL OPTIONS

The Magic Wand has one unique option setting: tolerance. By setting the tolerance, you can define how picky Photoshop will be in defining what colors are the same as the one you indicated (and, therefore, what will be included in the selection). The larger the number you enter, the more liberal its definition will be. A good place to start is at about 30. To make Photoshop define the color more liberally, enter a larger number. To make it define the color more precisely, enter a smaller number.

Often, you'll need to experiment to determine the value that works best. To do this, simply enter a value and click on the area you want to select. If you want to expand the area, enter a larger value, then click on the area again. If you want to reduce the area, enter a smaller value and click on the area again. Repeat this process as needed to find the value that produces the best results for the selection you want to make.

TIPS FOR USING THE MAGIC WAND TOOL

If the areas of identical color you want to select are not contiguous, uncheck the Contiguous box in the options palette.

Original color photograph.

Using the Magic Wand with the Tolerance set to 40, the red plates were selected.

With the selection still active, the Hue/Saturation tool was used to colorize the plates, rendering them blue.

SELECT A **COLOR RANGE**

▶ WHAT IT IS

The Color Range selection feature allows you to pick all the tones, throughout the frame, that fall within a given color range. This is similar to using the Magic Wand with the Contiguous box unchecked (see page 56), but with refined options for controlling the selection.

▶ HOW TO DO IT

Unlike the selection tools covered so far, this feature is accessed through a dialogue box. To open the dialogue box, go to Select>Color Range.

From here, you have many options. Begin at the top of the palette with the Select pull-down menu. Choose a color (reds, yellows, blues, cyans, greens, magentas) or tonal range (highlights, midtones, or shadows) from this list. As you do so, note the changes in the preview of the image (make sure this is set to Selection, using the radio buttons directly beneath the preview). The areas that are white are the ones that are selected. The areas in black are not selected.

Picking a color from the Select list can be useful for some images. If you're working with photographs, however, most areas aren't easily divided into a single color. Instead, you'll want to set the Select pull-down menu to Sampled Colors.

With Sampled Colors selected, move your cursor over the main image (not the preview in the Color Range dialogue box). You'll see that it is now shaped like an eyedropper, rather than the usual arrow. By clicking on an area in your image, you can sample the precise color in that area. As you do so, note the changes in the preview of the image (again, make sure this is set to Selection, using the radio buttons directly beneath the preview). The areas that are white are the ones that are selected. The areas in black are not selected.

Use the pull-down menu to indicate whether you want to select a color manually (based on a sample) or select an established color from the list (reds, yellows, blues, cyans, greens, magentas). You can also select the highlight, midtone, or shadow areas from this list.

Like the Tolerance setting on the Magic Wand tool (see page 56), the Fuzziness setting on the Color Range tool determines how discriminating Photoshop will be in its interpretation of your color. At lower settings, it will be very picky and look for more precise matches. At higher settings, it will be more liberal and allow for more variation.

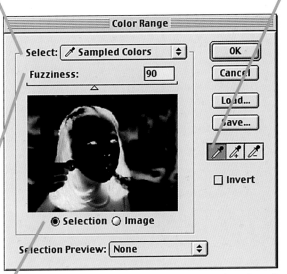

These options determine how you pick colors. The left eyedropper selects one color. The middle eyedropper (+) selects a color in addition to the previous color(s). The right eyedropper (−) removes a color from the previously selected color(s). Remember, the setting of the Fuzziness slider also influences how the colors are selected.

Choosing Selection allows you to view the selected area (the white areas). Choosing Image allows you to see your original image.

Next, experiment with the Fuzziness slider. Moving it to the right (higher value) makes more areas appear white (more areas are selected). Moving it to the left (lower value) makes fewer areas appear white (fewer areas are selected).

▶ EYEDROPPER TOOLS

Often, selecting just one tone won't completely select the area you want (or it may select too much). In these cases, use the eyedropper tools located below the save button.

The first eyedropper (left) selects one single color. The middle eyedropper (+) selects a color in addition to the previous color(s). The right eyedropper (−) removes a color from the previously selected color(s). Remember, the setting of the Fuzziness slider also influences how the colors are selected.

Once the white area in the preview image seems to encompass the area you want to select, hit OK.

Original photograph (courtesy of Ron Nichols).

With the Select menu set to Sampled Colors, the eyedropper tool was clicked on the girl's dark hair. The Fuzziness slider was adjusted until the desired area was selected.

All of the dark tones were selected—the girl's hair, eyes and eyebrows.

MORE ON SELECTIONS

▶ DON'T GIVE UP

You've now learned the most basic tools used to make selections. The next chapter covers the interaction of these tools, their settings, and a few additional selection functions. Rarely is one tool used to make a complete selection. So, if you're feeling frustrated, read on. The solution probably rests in strategically combining tools and functions.

WORKING WITH SELECTIONS

IMPORTANT TERMS

Add—To include additional image areas in a selection.

Feather—To blur the edges of a selection.

Inverse—To select all of the areas in an image that were *excluded* from the base selection.

Subtract—To remove some image areas from a selection.

ADDING TO AND SUBTRACTING FROM SELECTIONS

▶ WHAT IT MEANS

Regardless of how careful or precise you are, you'll rarely make a perfect selection on your first try. If you use the Lasso tool, you'll go slightly outside or inside the lines. If you use the Magic Wand, you'll end up with a ragged edge on your selection (or selecting an area you don't want to select). Fortunately, many problems can be fixed by adding to or subtracting from your selection.

If your selection (as it stands) *missed* an area you wanted to include, you'll need to add to your selection. If your selection *included* an area you didn't want to include, you'll need to subtract from your selection.

selection. It's okay if the new area overlaps the previously selected areas; the overlaps will be combined in the resulting new selection.

The original selection, made with the Magic Wand (left) included areas outside the lightbulb. Using the Polygonal Lasso set to subtract (middle) the extraneous material was removed (right).

The original selection with the Magic Wand (left) didn't include the shirt's pink trim. Using the Magic Wand set to add (middle), the area was included. The Lasso tool (set as needed) was used to clean up the selection (right).

▶ HOW TO ADD TO A SELECTION

Choose a selection tool from the toolbar. (Which tool you select will depend on the refinements you want to make.) In the options palette, click on the "Add to Selection" icon. A small "+" will appear next to your cursor as you move over the image, indicating that you are now adding to the selection.

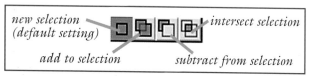

new selection (default setting) · add to selection · intersect selection · subtract from selection

Apply the selected tool as described on pages 54–56, selecting the area you want to add to your

▶ HOW TO SUBTRACT FROM A SELECTION

Choose a selection tool from the toolbar. In the options palette, click on the "Subtract from Selection" icon. A small "−" will appear next to your cursor as you move over the image, indicating that you are now subtracting from the selection. Apply the selected tool as described on pages 54–56, selecting the area you want to remove from your selection. Be careful to select *only* the areas you want to remove.

INVERSING SELECTIONS

▶ WHAT IT MEANS

Inversing a selection allows you to apply the selection tools (alone or in combination), then automatically select all of the areas in your photo that are *not* in that originally selected area. There are two common scenarios in which you might want to use this technique.

First, you may have an image where you want to make one type of correction to one particular area, then another correction to the rest of the photo. For example, you might have a portrait that, overall, needs only small color corrections—except for the subject's shirt, which you'd really like to change to another color. You could select the shirt, change the color, then invert the selection (selecting everything *except* the shirt), and make the rest of your changes.

Second, in some instances it may be easiest to select the material you *don't* want to include in the selection, then invert the selection to include the areas you *do* want. Consider the example below of a colorful leaf against a white background. To select the leaf, you could trace its outline with the Lasso tool, or use the Magic Wand to select each tone. A better solution, however, would be to use the Magic Wand to select the white area around the leaf, then invert the selection to include everything *except* the white area (namely, the leaf).

▶ HOW TO INVERSE A SELECTION

Make a selection using the techniques described on pages 54–60. As noted above, select the areas you do *not* want in your final selection. Then, go to Select>Inverse to deselect these areas and automatically select all other areas in the image.

To quickly select the leaf itself, first select the white area around the leaf. Since this is all one tone, it is easy to select with the Magic Wand.

With the white area selected, go to Select>Inverse. This will leave you with everything except *the white area selected—namely, the entire leaf.*

FEATHERING SELECTIONS

▶ WHAT IT MEANS

When using the selection tools to make a selection, you may notice that the edges of the selected area are very hard and abrupt. In photos, where tones normally blend into one another to some degree, this can make the edges of your selection look unnatural—as though they were cut with a pair of scissors. Feathering a selection allows you to slightly (or dramatically) blur the edges of the selected area, creating a smoother look.

▶ HOW TO DO IT

With your selection made (and still active with the dotted black & white line surrounding it), go to Select>Feather. Doing this will cause the Feather Selection dialogue box to appear. In this box, you will need to enter a number. The larger the number you supply, the more the edges of the selection will be blurred. Deciding exactly what number to enter will take some experimentation.

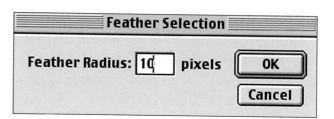

Feather Selection dialogue box. The larger the number, the more the edges of the selection will be blurred.

In general, 2 pixels will create an edge that is barely blurred—just enough to create a smooth transition, but not enough to be noticeable to the viewer. Ten or more pixels of blurring will be very soft and blurred (see the examples below).

For more on the practical applications of feathering a selection, turn to page 118. Here, you will learn how to seamlessly composite (combine elements from two or more images) photographs. For this technique, feathered selections are used to create edges that blend realistically with other elements in the image.

Original photograph (courtesy of Ron Nichols).

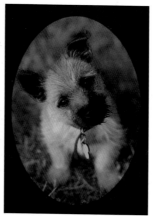

To create a vignette (dark area around the edges), the Elliptical Marquee tool was used to select an oval area around the subject. This selection was then inversed (see page 61) and filled with black set to 50% opacity (Edit>Fill). The selection was not feathered.

Here, the same steps were followed, except that the selection was feathered 20 pixels before being filled with black. As a result, the edges of the selection look soft and blurred, creating a more gradual and natural transition.

Again, the same steps were followed, but the selection was feathered 40 pixels before being filled with black. As a result, the edges of the selection are even more soft and blurred.

MODIFYING **SELECTIONS**

▶ WHAT IT MEANS

Photoshop offers several automated tools for adjusting your selections. These allow you to smooth, expand, or contract an existing selection—or create an outline based on it.

▶ HOW TO DO IT

With a selection made (and still active with the dotted black & white line surrounding it), go to Select>Modify and choose the option you want (Border, Expand, Contract, or Smooth). In the dialogue box that appears, select the degree of change by entering a number of pixels (the higher the number, the greater the change). Experimenting with the settings will give you a good idea of what to anticipate (and a few examples are shown below). Smoothing a selection by one or two pixels can be particularly useful—especially if you don't have a perfectly steady hand when using the Lasso tool.

Initial selection made using the Lasso tool. (Original photograph courtesy of Ron Nichols.)

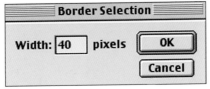

Border Selection dialogue box (bottom) and selection modification applied (top).

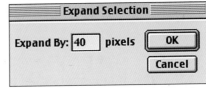

Expand Selection dialogue box (bottom) and selection modification applied (top).

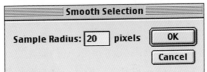

Smooth Selection dialogue box (bottom) and selection modification applied (top).

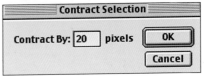

Contract Selection dialogue box (bottom) and selection modification applied (top).

GROW

► WHAT IT MEANS

The Grow command, as the name implies, allows you to increase an already selected area. It does this by causing the selection to expand to the next logical stage. This is similar to the effect of adding to the selection with the Magic Wand, and like the Magic Wand it will add to the selection by including similar tones in contiguous areas.

► HOW TO DO IT

To begin, make a selection using the methods described on pages 54–58. To apply the Grow command, go to Select>Grow. The selection will grow automatically. You can do this repeatedly to make your selection grow incrementally larger.

This can be a very useful technique when selecting an area with somewhat varied tones—especially when that area would be hard to select with another tool. The example shown below is such a scenario. Here, the clothes contain various tones—whites, pale bluish shadows, and light pinks from the setting sun. All are in the same tonal range, however. By selecting an area with the Magic Wand, then using the Grow command, many of these tones can be quickly added to the selection. To continue adding to the selection, use the techniques presented on page 60. Keep in mind that you can use the Grow command after each step.

Right: *Original photograph (courtesy of Ron Nichols).*

Bottom, Left: *The initial selection was made using the Magic Wand.*

Bottom, Right: *The Grow command was used to expand the selection to the next logical step, encompassing additional contiguous tones that are similar to the one in the original selection.*

SIMILAR

Original selection made with the Magic Wand.

Using the Similar command, the selection is expanded.

Using the Similar command multiple times, the selection is expanded even further.

▶ WHAT IT MEANS

The Similar command, like the Grow tool, allows you to add to your selection. Rather than adding similar contiguous tones, the Similar command seeks out similar tones throughout the image and adds them to your selection.

▶ HOW TO DO IT

To begin, make a selection using the methods described on pages 54–58. To use the Similar command, go to Select>Similar. The selection will grow automatically. You can do this repeatedly to make your selection grow incrementally larger and larger.

This can be a very useful technique when selecting an area that is (in terms of its tonality) unique within an image—especially when that area would be hard to select with another tool. The example shown to the left is such an example. Here, the clothes are the only white (or very light) area in the photograph. By selecting one of these areas with the Magic Wand, then using the Similar command, many of these tones can be quickly added to the selection.

To continue adding to the selection, use the techniques presented on page 60. Keep in mind that you can use the Similar command after each step. You can also use the Grow command together with the Similar command as needed.

SAVE/LOAD SELECTION

▶ WHAT IT MEANS

By now, you've probably noticed that making selections can be pretty complicated business. To make things worse, it's all too easy to accidentally deactivate a selection. Therefore, Photoshop offers you the opportunity to save your selections—then you can load (reactivate) them as needed. It's a good idea to save your selection whenever you make a complicated one.

▶ HOW TO SAVE A SELECTION

With your selection active, go to Select>Save Selection. A dialogue box like the one shown below will open up. Next to Document, you should see the name of the file you are working on. Leave the Channel pull-down set to New. Next to Name, type a quick description of the selection (here, "shirt"). Under Operation, leave the New Channel radio button checked. Finally, hit OK to save the selection.

▶ HOW TO LOAD A SELECTION

Once you have saved the selection, return to your document and deactivate the selection by clicking anywhere on the image with the Marquee tool (make sure the tool is set to New Selection in the tool options; to review this, turn to page 60).

Once the selection is deactivated, go to Select> Load Selection. Doing so will cause a dialogue box like the one shown below to appear. In this box, you will see your document name at the top. Under Channel, you should see the name you entered when you saved the selection. (On some occasions, you may want to save more than one selection per image. In this case, pull down on the Channel menu and select the particular one you want to load.) Under Operation, leave the New Selection radio button checked. Finally, hit OK to load the selection.

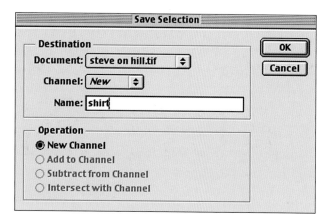

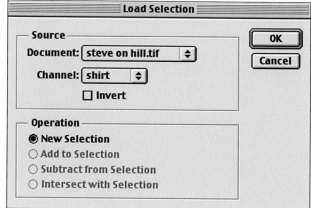

RECOVERING LOST SELECTIONS

Invariably, from time to time, you will accidentally deactivate a selection. If that happens, immediately go to Edit>Undo Deselect to restore the selection. (You must do this immediately, as Edit>Undo only allows you to undo the very last thing you did.)

If you don't catch the error immediately, turn to pages 96–97 to learn how to use the history palette. With this tool, you can essentially turn back time—and move back to a point before your selection became accidentally deactivated.

SELECTIONS
IN ACTION

IMPORTANT TERMS

Fill—To apply a color, pattern, or other data to an entire selected area.

Pattern—A repeated sequence of image data that can be applied as fill data.

Stroke—The creation of a geometric line surrounding a selection.

COLOR ENHANCEMENT

▶ WHAT IT MEANS

Once you've learned to use selections, you'll be amazed at how many additional options you have for perfecting your photographs (or other artwork). In particular, color correction can be dramatically improved by making selective (rather than universal) changes. Additionally, you can enhance color in creative ways using selections. The following are a few ideas to get you started.

▶ CREATIVE COLORATION

In this technique, you will select one area to leave in color, but make the rest of the photo black & white.

1. Begin with a photograph in the RGB color mode.

Right: *Original photograph (courtesy of Jeff Hawkins).*

Below: *Final enhanced photo.*

2. Carefully select the area you wish to have remain in color.

3. Go to Select>Inverse to inverse the selection (review this process on page 61).

4. Under Select>Feather, enter 2 pixels (review this process on page 62).

5. Go to Image>Adjustments>Hue/Saturation. Activate the Colorize feature and set the Saturation and Lightness to 0 (the hue setting won't matter). Hit OK to apply the change. (To review this tool, see pages 46–47.)

6. Deactivate the selection by clicking anywhere on the image with the Marquee tool (making sure the tool is set to New Selection in the tool options [see page 60]).

▶ SELECTIVE COLOR ENHANCEMENT

In this technique, you will select one area to adjust, but leave all the other areas in the photograph untouched.

1. Begin with a photograph in the RGB color mode.

2. Carefully select the area where you wish to refine the color.

3. Under Select>Feather, enter 2 pixels (review this process on page 62).

4. Using any of the color correction tools (see pages 18–23 and 40–48 to review the usage of these tools), enhance the color of the selected area(s) as you like.

5. Deactivate the selection by clicking anywhere on the image with the Marquee tool (make

Right: *Original photograph (almost-ripe tomato too yellow).*

Below: *Final enhanced photo.*

sure the tool is set to New Selection in the tool options; to review this, turn to page 60).

In the example shown above, an RGB image was used. In it, the almost-ripe tomatoes were a little too yellow. To change this, the Curves tool was used. After selecting the red channel, the center of the line was pulled up (creating an upward bend in the line). Because this was done with the selection active, the change affected only the selected areas (not the green foliage, which would have suffered from adding a red cast).

▶ SELECTIVE COLOR CHANGE

In this technique, you will select one area and completely change the color in it while leaving all the other areas in the photograph untouched.

1. Begin with a photograph in the RGB color mode.

2. Carefully select the area where you wish to refine the color.

3. Under Select>Feather, enter 2 pixels (review this process on page 62).

4. Using any of the color correction tools (see pages 18–23 and 40–48 to review the usage of these tools), enhance the color of the selected area(s) as you like—be sure to use extreme settings to produce the greatest possible alterations.

In the example shown below, the alligator was selected using the Lasso tool. The same tool was then set to Deselect to remove the creature's teeth from the selection so they would not change color. After feathering the selection, the Curves controls were used. Some experimentation within the channels—creating very steep or shallow curves, very wavy curves, etc.—produced the turquoise color that was finally selected. It's not a natural-looking effect, but it certainly is eye-catching!

Right: *Original photograph.*

Below: *Final enhanced photo.*

STROKE

▶ WHAT IT MEANS

Stroking is essentially the outlining of a selection. This is an easy way to draw a geometric line around an area in order to accent it, or even to create a "frame" around an entire image.

▶ HOW TO DO IT

To begin, simply make a selection. Then, go to Edit>Stroke. Doing so will cause the following dialogue box to appear.

In Width, enter the width of the line you want to create. The width is measured in pixels (5 will give you a thin line and over 10 will create a relatively thick line—try a few variations). In the color section, if you don't like the color displayed, click on it to activate the Color Picker and select a new color (to learn how to use the Color Picker, turn to page 75). Under Location, select whether you want the line to be drawn on the outer edge of the selected area (outside), on the inner edge of the selected area (inside), or centered on the dotted line that denotes the selected area. Under Blending, you can choose to alter the Mode or the Opacity of the effect. You can experiment with these settings (just go to Edit>Undo if you don't

like the results), or turn to pages 89–90 to learn precisely how to use these settings.

In the photo below, an oval was selected and a ten-point stroke was added in white. Then, the selection was inversed (Select>Inverse). With the outer edges of the photo now selected, the contrast was reduced (Image>Adjustments>Brightness/Contrast) and the Sprayed Strokes filter was applied (Filter>Brush Strokes>Sprayed Strokes). The result is a unique framing effect.

Right: *Original photograph.*

Below: *Enhanced photo.*

so there are three sliders—red, green, and blue. To the left of the sliders are two swatches that correspond to the current foreground (top, left) and background (bottom, right) colors. At the bottom of the window is a gradient bar of colors with swatches for pure white and pure black at the far right.

To choose a color, click to select the foreground or background swatch in this window. (The swatch with the white line around it is the active one, and the one you will be changing.) Then, if you see a spot on the gradient bar that is close to the color you want, click on it. From there, you can adjust the sliders for each channel until you get the color just right. If you prefer, you can skip clicking on the gradient bar and just adjust the sliders.

▶ USING THE COLOR PICKER

To activate the Color Picker, go to the toolbar and click once on either the foreground or background color swatch.

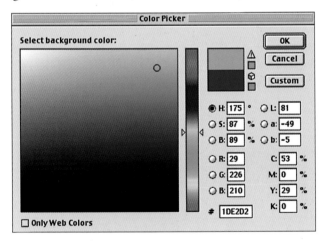

Here, you will see a large window with shades of a single color. To the right of this window is a narrow gradient bar with the full spectrum of colors. At the top right are two swatches; at the top is the current color, and at the bottom is the original color. At the bottom right are the numerical "recipes" for the selected color (for more on this, read the following section on the info palette).

To use the Color Picker, begin with the narrow gradient bar. Click and slowly drag the slider on the side of the bar up and down until you see something close to the color you want in the large window. Then, in that large window, position your cursor over the color you want and click to select it. Hit OK to apply the change.

▶ USING THE INFO PALETTE

The info palette (Window>Info) is a great source of information about the colors already in your image. To use it, position your cursor over a color in your image, then look at the info palette.

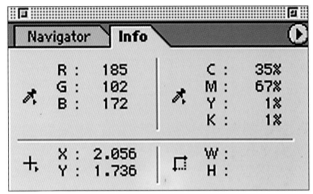

In the RGB (or CMYK) section, you'll see the "recipe" for this color—the mix of component colors used to create this particular tone. If you want to remember that color for the future, copy down the recipe (for example, R=185, G=102, B=172). You can then enter this information in the Color Palette (in the white boxes to the right of the sliders) or in the Color Picker (in the white boxes to the right of the narrow gradient bar) to reliably create the identical color.

EYEDROPPER TOOL

To quickly set the foreground color to match an existing color in your image, select the eyedropper tool (see page 50). Then, move the tool over the color you want to match and click it. Your foreground color will be set to precisely the same color.

BRUSH SELECTION

▶ WHAT IT MEANS

Brush selection determines how color is applied by tools like the Brush and Pencil tools (see page 50). You can choose large brushes for big areas, or small brushes for fine details. You can also choose how soft (blurry) or hard (crisp) the brush is.

▶ BRUSHES PALETTE

To begin, select the Brush tool (see page 50) and look at the options palette (see page 77). To see the brushes palette, click on the downward pointing arrow at the edge of the brushes area of the options palette (segment shown below).

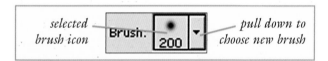

selected brush icon — Brush. 200 — *pull down to choose new brush*

In the brushes menu (below), you can select a brush by simply clicking on the one you want. You can also use the Master Diameter slider to make it bigger or smaller. Often, you'll find you want to create a new brush tailored to your needs—so read on for tips on customizing brushes.

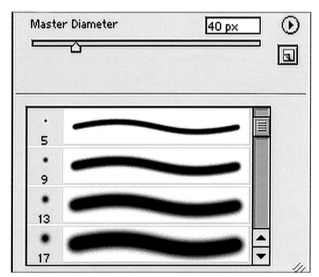

▶ BRUSH OPTIONS

You can also customize your brushes by adjusting the brush options (the parameters that control the character of the line drawn by a brush). These are:

Diameter—How wide the brush is.

Hardness—How soft or hard an edge the brush paints (0% is very soft, 100% is very hard).

Spacing—How mouse speed affects the individual "paint" drops. With spacing at about 25%, you can paint a fairly smooth line. Experiment with different values and with the spacing clicked off and you'll quickly see the effect.

Angle—With a brush that is not 100% round, this sets the angle at which the brush is "held."

Roundness—Lets you to create oval brushes.

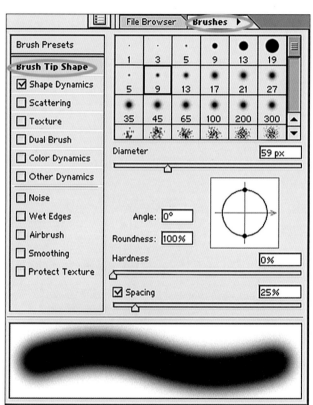

To access the brushes palette, go to the Brushes tab at the top right of your screen (if your window does not look like the one above, click on the black triangle on the right side of the Brushes tab and select Expanded View). From the list on the left side of the window, select Brush Tip Shape. In the window above the sliders, locate a brush that looks close to what you want and click on it. Then, use the sliders to edit the brush as you like.

Check out the other settings in the left column of this window and experiment with their effects. For example, with the Wet Edges setting activated (below) you can create a brush that applies your digital "paint" a little differently.

BRUSH TOOL

▶ WHAT IT IS

The Brush tool applies color as you would apply paint to a canvas.

▶ HOW TO USE IT

Set the foreground color, then choose the Brush tool from the toolbar (see page 50). In the options palette, select the desired brush, then click and hold to paint as you move the mouse.

▶ OPTIONS

The Mode option allows you to choose how the "paint" interacts with the colors under it. For an overview of modes, see page 89. The opacity controls how much "paint" is applied; 100% opacity lays down an opaque layer, while lower settings create more transparent looks. In one pass (or stroke) of the brush, the paint applied will never exceed this opacity, so you can create a very even application.

You can also activate the airbrush setting (far right of the options palette) and adjust the flow setting. At less than 100% flow, the paint will build up as you move your brush back and forth over an area (as if you were using an airbrush).

Brush tool options.

PENCIL TOOL

▶ WHAT IT IS

The Pencil draws hard-edged lines.

▶ HOW TO USE IT

Set the foreground color, then choose the Pencil tool from the toolbar (see page 50). In the options palette, select the desired brush (only hard brushes will be available). Move your cursor over your image, then click and hold to paint as you move the mouse.

▶ OPTIONS

The option settings are basically identical to those of the Brush (see above). The one exception is the Auto Erase option. This is a tricky tool—*approach with caution*! To employ it, use the Eyedropper tool to select a foreground and background color from your image. Activate the Auto Erase function on the Pencil tool. If you begin erasing over a pixel of the foreground color, the background color will be applied. If you begin erasing over a pixel of the background color, the foreground color will be applied.

CLONE AND PATTERN STAMP TOOLS

▶ CLONE STAMP: WHAT IT MEANS

The Clone Stamp is like a rubber stamp. It creates an invisible duplicate of your image that is centered on a reference point (or "sample") that you specify. Centering on this sample, you can then "stamp" the pixels from this duplicate onto another part of your image. This can be useful for removing small objects from a photo, or for eliminating dust and scratches from a scanned image.

▶ CLONE STAMP: HOW TO DO IT

Select the Clone Stamp tool from the toolbar (see page 50), then select a brush. Hold down the Alt/Opt key, then move your cursor over the area you want to clone and click once (with the Alt/Opt key depressed, your cursor should look like a little rubber stamp). Release the Alt/Opt key and move your cursor to the area where you want to stamp, and click once (or click and drag).

▶ CLONE STAMP: ACCURATE SAMPLING

There are two keys to a seamless effect: choose a slightly soft brush and sample accurately. When selecting an area to sample, look for one that is as close as possible in tone and texture to the area you want to stamp over. It may take some practice to identify these areas accurately. You can stamp as many times as you want from a single sample, but read through the following section first.

▶ CLONE STAMP: OPTIONS

The Clone Stamp tool has basically the same options as the Brush tool (refer to page 77). The Aligned option, however, is an important addition. With the Aligned option activated, when you start stamping, the originally sampled reference point remains static. If you stamp once, you'll

apply the image data from the original reference point. If you stamp a second time 2" to the left, you'll apply the image data from 2" to the left of the original reference point. With the aligned option *deactivated*, when you start stamping, the originally sampled reference point moves with each stamp you make. If you stamp once, you'll apply the image data from the original reference

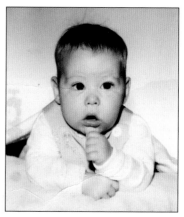

Right: *The original photograph had a number of deep scratches and discolored areas.*

Below: *With careful use of the Clone Stamp tool, areas of similar tone and texture were sampled and stamped over the problem areas.*

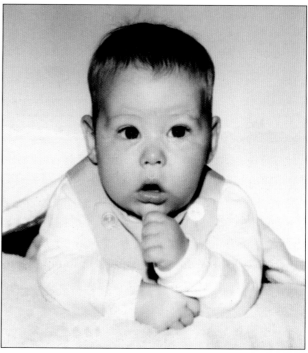

Clone Stamp tool options palette.

point. If you stamp a second time 2" to the left, you'll apply the data from the first reference point.

As you click to stamp, you'll also notice that a small "+" appears on your image. This "+" marks the spot from which the stamp tool is drawing the material it will apply when you click. If you keep an eye on this, you'll be able to make sure your stamp applies the tone you want. If it doesn't, go to Edit>Undo to reverse the last stamp.

▶ PATTERN STAMP: WHAT IT MEANS

The Pattern Stamp tool applies a predefined pattern to your image. This pattern can be one of the patterns that is packaged with Photoshop, or it can be one that you establish yourself.

▶ PATTERN STAMP: HOW TO DO IT

Select the Pattern Stamp tool (see page 50), then select a brush. Move your cursor to the area where you want to stamp, then click or click and drag.

▶ PATTERN STAMP: OPTIONS

The Pattern Stamp tool has basically the same options as the Clone Stamp tool. Once you have determined the desired settings, simply pull down

on the Pattern menu and select the pattern you want to use.

▶ DEFINING A PATTERN

Setting your own pattern is very easy. Simply select an area of an image (or an entire image). With the selection active, go to Edit>Define Pattern. Doing so will open a window like the one shown below.

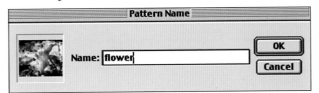

When this appears, enter a name for the pattern and click OK. The new pattern will now appear in the pattern menu for all tools that offer the option to use a pattern.

GET IT STRAIGHT

By holding down the Shift key while drawing/painting you can create neat, straight lines that run vertically, horizontally or at a 45° angle. This technique works with the Brush, Pencil, Clone Stamp, Pattern Stamp, and Eraser tools.

HEALING BRUSH **TOOL**

▶ WHAT IT IS

The Healing Brush tool works pretty much like the Clone tool—you sample (Opt/Alt + click) and stamp (click or click and drag) to conceal problem areas. The benefit of using the Healing Brush is that it works to seamlessly blend the stamped data with the underlying image.

▶ HOW TO DO IT

Because it blends your image data for you, the Healing Brush tool is great for eliminating blemishes on skin—or problems in other areas where fine details in color and texture might be compromised by stamping data on with the Clone tool.

▶ OPTIONS

The opacity of the Healing Brush tool is always 100%. You cannot adjust it. Additionally, brush selection and editing is available only from the pull-down menu just to the right of the tool icon in the options pallette.

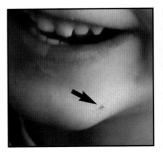

ERASER **TOOL**

▶ WHAT IT IS

The Eraser removes data from the image you are working on, much like a pencil eraser.

▶ HOW TO DO IT

Select the Eraser tool from the toolbar (see page 50). Select either the brush or pencil mode from the Mode pull-down menu, then choose a brush. Click (or click and drag) on your image to erase a desired area. Photoshop considers the background color to be what is "behind" your image, so this will begin to show through as you erase. (*Note:* If you have multiple layers in your image [see pages 86–88], erasing will reveal the layer below the one you are working on [or, if you are working on the bottom layer of the image, the background color].)

▶ OPTIONS

In the brush or pencil mode, the Eraser options are identical to the tool it is modeled on (i.e., the Brush or Pencil tool). In the Block mode, the Eraser becomes a square of a fixed size with 100% opacity. The Eraser tool also has an Erase to History feature, which allows you to turn back time in the area you are erasing. This function works almost identically to the History Brush, which will be discussed in chapter 11. When you have completed that chapter, you may wish to return to your study of the Eraser tool and experiment with this option.

PAINT BUCKET **TOOL**

▶ WHAT IT IS

The Paint Bucket tool pours paint into any area you select.

▶ HOW TO DO IT

Select the Paint Bucket from the toolbar (see page 50). To fill an area with a solid color, set the foreground color (see pages 74–75), then select Foreground from the Fill menu in the tool options. To fill an area with a pattern, select Pattern from the Fill menu in the tool options, then select the desired pattern from the Pattern pull-down menu. Finally, click on the area you want to fill.

▶ OPTIONS

The Paint Bucket works outward from the point you click on, stopping when it finds a different color, the edge of a selection, or the edge of an image. Under Tolerance, you can define how picky Photoshop will be in defining what colors are the same as the one you indicated (and, therefore, what will be filled). The larger the number you enter, the more liberal its definition will be. If you click Anti-Aliased, Photoshop will smooth the edges of your fill area (preventing jagged edges to some degree). If you *deactivate* the Contiguous option, Photoshop will look throughout the frame for identical colors to fill. If you choose All Layers, Photoshop will take into consideration the data on other layers when applying the fill (see chapter 10 to learn how to use layers, then return to experiment with this technique). (The Mode and Opacity settings for the Paint Bucket are used in the same way as for the Brush tool [see page 77].)

GRADIENT **TOOL**

▶ WHAT IT IS

The Gradient tool allows you to fill an area with a transitional blend of two or more colors.

▶ HOW TO DO IT

Select the Gradient tool from the toolbar (see page 50), then click anywhere on your image and drag away from the point a couple of inches (more or less is fine). Release your mouse button, and the gradient will appear across the entire image. (You can perform the same function on discrete parts of your image by selecting the area where you want the gradient, then applying it as described above.)

▶ OPTIONS

In this palette (seen directly below), you will determine the style of the gradient and the colors used in it. Pull down on the arrow to the right of the colored window showing the currently selected gradient to reveal Photoshop's preset gradients.

If you like, you can select one of these by clicking on it. To the right on the options palette are five boxes that allow you to select the pattern for your gradient (linear, radial, angle, reflected or diamond). A quick test of each will familiarize you with their functions. Next are the Mode and Opacity settings (refer to pages 89–90 for information on these). At the far right of the palette are settings for: Reverse (flips the colors of the gradient from left to right), Dither (helps reduce the appearance of banding [stripes] in the gradient), and Transparency (enables any transparency that is edited into the gradient in the Gradient Editor dialogue box).

If you'd prefer to create your own gradient, click once on the current gradient in the options palette. Doing so will open the Gradient Editor dialogue box (seen at the bottom of this page). Refer to the box below to learn its functions.

Gradient tool options.

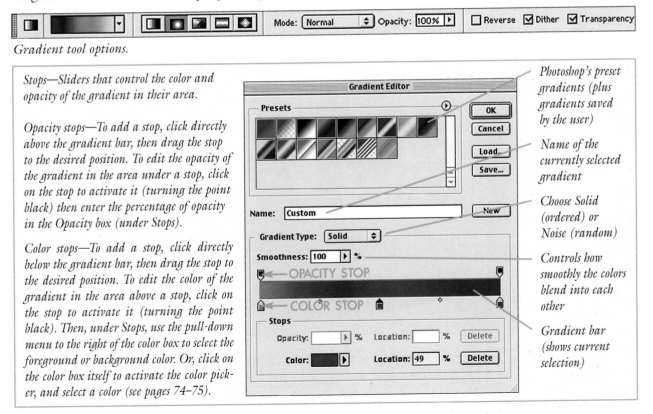

Stops—Sliders that control the color and opacity of the gradient in their area.

Opacity stops—To add a stop, click directly above the gradient bar, then drag the stop to the desired position. To edit the opacity of the gradient in the area under a stop, click on the stop to activate it (turning the point black) then enter the percentage of opacity in the Opacity box (under Stops).

Color stops—To add a stop, click directly below the gradient bar, then drag the stop to the desired position. To edit the color of the gradient in the area above a stop, click on the stop to activate it (turning the point black). Then, under Stops, use the pull-down menu to the right of the color box to select the foreground or background color. Or, click on the color box itself to activate the color picker, and select a color (see pages 74–75).

Photoshop's preset gradients (plus gradients saved by the user)

Name of the currently selected gradient

Choose Solid (ordered) or Noise (random)

Controls how smoothly the colors blend into each other

Gradient bar (shows current selection)

SHARPEN/BLUR/SMUDGE TOOL

▶ SHARPEN: WHAT IT MEANS

The Sharpen tool, unlike the sharpen filters (see pages 34–35), allows you to paint on "sharpness" only where you want it.

▶ SHARPEN: HOW TO DO IT

Select the Sharpen tool from the toolbar (see page 50), then choose a brush (a soft brush works best). Click (or click and drag) over your image to sharpen as needed. In the options palette, increasing the pressure will increase the sharpness. For an overview of modes, turn to page 89.

▶ BLUR: WHAT IT MEANS

The Blur tool, unlike the blur filters (see page 28), allows you to paint on a blurred effect only where you want it.

▶ BLUR: HOW TO DO IT

Select the Blur tool from the toolbar (see page 50), and choose a brush (a soft brush works best). Then click (or click and drag) over your image to blur as needed. In the options palette, increasing the pressure will increase the bluriness. For an overview of modes, turn to page 89.

▶ SMUDGE: WHAT IT MEANS

The Smudge tool lets you displace parts of your image—much like running your fingers across a wet painting.

▶ SMUDGE: HOW TO DO IT

Select the Smudge tool from the toolbar (see page 50), and choose a brush (of any hardness). Then click and drag across your image to smudge the colors. In the options palette, increasing the pressure will increase the smudge (this is like pressing harder and deeper into the wet paint). For an overview of modes, turn to page 89.

In the original image (left) the background was so sharp that it distracted from the calf. To make the calf stand out better, the Blur tool was used to soften the background area just enough to make it look out of focus.

Sharpen tool options.

Blur tool options.

Smudge tool options.

▶ WHAT IT MEANS

The Dodge tool is named (and modeled) after a traditional darkroom technique used to lighten select areas of a print. As light hits photographic paper, it gets darker, so dodging (preventing light from hitting an area) reduces the darkness there. The same idea applies in Photoshop, although the controls are much more precise.

▶ HOW TO DO IT

Select the Dodge tool from the toolbar (see page 50), then choose a brush (a soft brush works best). Click (or click and drag) over your image to dodge (lighten) as needed.

▶ OPTIONS

In the options palette, increasing the Exposure setting will increase the amount of lightening you achieve. In the Range setting, you can specify whether you want to lighten the shadows, midtones, or highlights in a given area. This is an important decision, so be sure to study the area you are working on carefully to determine the best approach. Often, the best selection is counter-intuitive. For example, imagine you have a photograph with a dark shadow area. The area is not solid black, but has very dark gray details. To bring out the details, it might seem logical to dodge the shadows. However, in this case, dodging the shadow areas would mean lightening the black areas, making them gray. If the shadow area and its details are *both* gray, then the contrast between them has actually been reduced, making the details even less visible. Instead, you would want to dodge the *midtones,* to lighten the areas that were originally *dark gray.* Making those gray areas a little lighter will make them more apparent to the viewer.

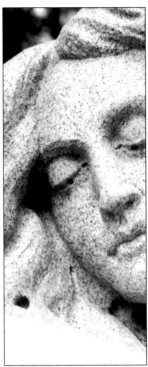

Original photograph.   *Photograph with 20% exposure dodge on midtones.*

RULE OF THUMB

You'll rarely get good results dodging a solid black (or extremely dark) area. If a black area has some detail in it (lighter areas that reveal the texture of the subject), try setting the Dodge tool's Range to Midtone or Highlight and lightening those details. Similarly, when burning (covered on page 84), you'll rarely get good results working on a solid white (or extremely light) area. If a white area has some detail in it (darker areas that reveal the texture of the subject), try setting the Burn tool's Range to Midtone or Shadow and darkening those details.

BURN TOOL

▶ WHAT IT MEANS

The Burn tool is named (and modeled) after a traditional darkroom technique used to darken select areas of a print. As light hits photographic paper, it gets darker, so burning (letting more light hit an area) increases the darkness there. The same idea applies in Photoshop, although the controls are much more precise.

▶ HOW TO DO IT

Select the Burn tool from the toolbar (see page 50), then choose a brush (a soft brush works best). Click (or click and drag) over your image to burn (darken) as needed.

▶ OPTIONS

In the options palette, increasing the Exposure setting will increase the amount of darkening you achieve. In the Range setting, you can choose to darken the shadows, midtones, or highlights in a given area. This is an important decision, so study the area you are working on carefully to determine the best approach. Often, the best selection is counterintuitive. For example, imagine you have a photograph with a bright highlight area. The area is not solid white, but has very light gray details. To bring out the details, it seems it would be logical to burn the highlights. However, in this case, burning the highlight areas would mean darkening the white areas, making them light gray. If the highlight area and its details are *both* light gray, then the contrast between them has actually been reduced, making the details even less visible. Instead, you would want to burn the midtones or shadows to make the areas that were originally light gray become somewhat darker. This will make them more apparent to the viewer of the image.

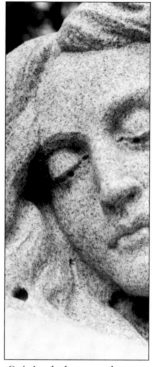 

Original photograph.   *Photograph with 20% exposure burn on midtones.*

SMALL CHANGES ARE BEST

Neither dodging nor burning can add detail that isn't in the original image (i.e., if a shadow is solid black, you can make it a lighter gray, but you can't recapture texture that wasn't in the image to begin with). Dodging and burning are most useful for making small changes, such as opening up a shaded area that's just a little too dark, or making an area that is too light just a little less bright and distracting.

WORKING
WITH LAYERS

WHAT **LAYERS** ARE

▶ WHAT IT MEANS

Layers are one of the most versatile tools in Photoshop. Essentially, layers are like sheets of clear plastic, laid one on top of the other. Each layer can be accessed, worked on, moved, added, or deleted independently of any other layer.

▶ WHY IT'S IMPORTANT

Using layers allows you to adjust and add to your image in a unique way. Because each layer you work on can be accessed without disturbing your other work, you can try out effects—and simply discard the layer if you don't like them. You can change the opacity of the layer to allow other layers to show through as much or as little as you want. You can also select from a variety of layer modes, which allow the layers to interact with each other in unique (and often beautiful) ways.

▶ LAYERS PALETTE

Layers are created, accessed, and manipulated via the layers palette (shown below). If this is not visible on your screen, go to Window>Layers. As you can see in the diagram, many features connected with the use of layers can be accessed directly from this palette. Other features for using layers are accessed via the Layers pull-down menu at the top of the screen.

The main feature in the layers palette is the list of layers in an image. These are stacked from bottom to top. In this case, the background layer is the bottom layer, layer 1 is on top of it, layer 2 is on top of that, and the text layer (here, containing the words "garden party") is the top layer.

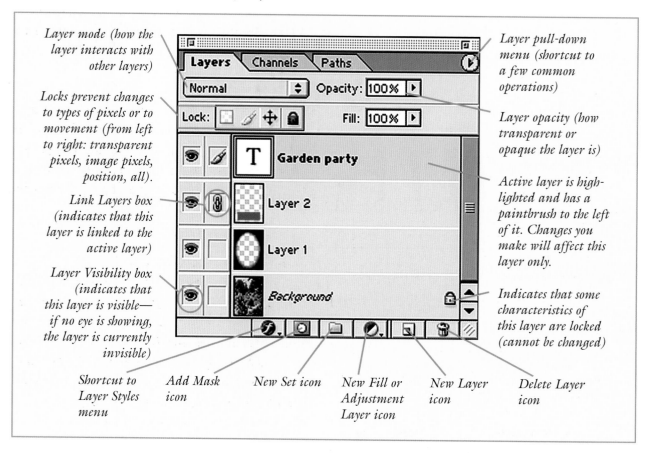

Layer mode (how the layer interacts with other layers)

Locks prevent changes to types of pixels or to movement (from left to right: transparent pixels, image pixels, position, all).

Link Layers box (indicates that this layer is linked to the active layer)

Layer Visibility box (indicates that this layer is visible— if no eye is showing, the layer is currently invisible)

Layer pull-down menu (shortcut to a few common operations)

Layer opacity (how transparent or opaque the layer is)

Active layer is highlighted and has a paintbrush to the left of it. Changes you make will affect this layer only.

Indicates that some characteristics of this layer are locked (cannot be changed)

Shortcut to Layer Styles menu

Add Mask icon

New Set icon

New Fill or Adjustment Layer icon

New Layer icon

Delete Layer icon

▶ WHAT IT MEANS

In an image, you can create as many layers as you like—but keep in mind that additional layers make images take up more memory. This means you'll need more space to store your image, and more time to open it or to perform operations on it.

▶ COPY/CUT AND PASTE

One way to automatically create a new layer is to make a selection, then go to Edit>Cut or Edit> Copy (cutting will remove the selected area, copying will duplicate it). Then, go to Edit>Paste. The material you select will reappear, but if you look at the layers palette, you will notice that it is in a new layer that can now be moved or edited independently. (To move the new layer, click on it once in the layers palette to activate it. Then, select the Move tool [see page 50]. Click and drag on the image to move the new layer and the material on it.)

▶ LAYER>NEW>LAYER

To create a new, empty layer, go to Layer>New >Layer. Alternately, from the upper-right corner of the layers palette, use the pull-down menu (from the arrow) and select New Layer. Doing so will cause the following dialogue box to appear.

New Layer	
Name: big flower	OK
☐ Group With Previous Layer	Cancel
Color: ☐ None ⬍	
Mode: Normal ⬍ Opacity: 100 ▶ %	
☐ (No neutral color exists for Normal mode.)	

At the top of this box is a blank space in which you can type a descriptive name for your new layer. If you don't want to name it yourself, Photoshop will label the new layers sequentially (Layer 1, Layer 2, etc.). Below this is a check box that allows you to group the layer with the previous layer— this will be covered on page 88. Next, you can

choose a Color for your new layer (this doesn't affect the look or behavior of the layer, but works like a highlighting pen to help you distinguish an important layer in the layers palette—maybe to remind you that you need to do something to it before finishing your work). Next to Modes, you'll find a pull-down menu listing numerous options; you'll find detailed information about each on page 89. Finally, you can set the Opacity of the layer (as you approach 0% the layer becomes more and more transparent). This will be covered in detail on page 90.

These settings aren't etched in stone—they can be changed later via the layers palette. To change the color marker or name of the layer, go to the upper-right corner of the layers palette and use the pull-down menu (from the arrow) to select Layer Properties. You can also rename a layer by double-clicking on the existing name in the layers palette, then typing in a new name over the old one.

▶ NEW LAYERS FROM THE LAYERS PALETTE

To skip having to make any decisions about naming and colors and whatnot, simply click on the New Layer icon at the bottom of the layers palette. A new layer will be created instantly and numbered for you. Its mode will be set to Normal and its Opacity will be 100%.

DUPLICATING LAYERS

Often, you may want to duplicate an existing layer. To do this, go to the layers palette and drag the existing layer onto the New Layer icon at the bottom right of the palette. (Be careful not to get it in the trash can—go to Edit>Undo immediately if this happens!) Your new layer will have the same name as the original, but with the word "copy" after it.

WORKING WITH LAYERS

▶ WHAT IT MEANS

As you work with layers, there are a number of operations you'll use time and time again. These are detailed below.

▶ LINKING/GROUPING

Often, it's helpful to group (or link) layers together. For instance, imagine that (for some reason) you have your subject's body on one layer and her head on another. They are perfectly lined up, but now you want to move them both 3" to the left. You could move them individually and realign them, or—better yet—you could group them. Then, when you move the head, the body will always come along with it (as well it should!).

To group two (or more) layers, choose one of the layers and click on it to activate it. Then, click the Link Layers box (see page 86) next to each layer to be grouped with the one you selected—a chain will appear in the box telling you it is linked. To ungroup any of the layers, click on the chain and it will disappear.

▶ MAKE VISIBLE/INVISIBLE

When you want to work on a layer without being distracted by image elements on other layers, you can simply make those layers temporarily invisible. To do so, click on the Layer Visibility box just to the left of the Link Layers box (see page 86). Doing so will make the eye icon disappear, indicating the layer is invisible. To make it visible again, simply click the Layer Visibility box again.

This technique is really helpful when the area you want to work on is partially obscured by image elements on a layer above it. Or, if you're trying to decide between two options for an image, you can execute each option on a separate level, then switch them on alternately to decide which one looks best.

▶ MOVING LAYERS FORWARD AND BACKWARD

The layers are listed from front to back in the layers palette (front layers at the top, back layers at the bottom). This is an unalterable arrangement.

However, you *can* move the layers around—for example, to put the top layer in a position third from the bottom, etc. The only restraint is that the background layer must remain the back layer (although you can duplicate it and put that *copy* wherever you want). Reordering the layers is simple. In the layers palette, just click on a layer and drag it until its outline is positioned between the two layers where you want it to fall. Release your mouse button and the layer will be moved into its new position.

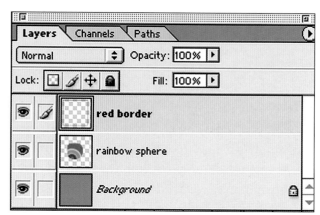

The top layer ("red border") was dragged so that it fell under the middle layer ("rainbow sphere") on the list.

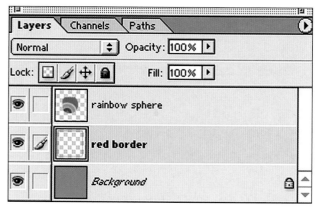

Because it is lower on the list, the "red border" layer is now behind the "rainbow sphere" layer.

LAYER MODES

The layer modes are a predetermined set of instructions for how the layers should interact with each other. The best way to learn about these is to try them—you may be surprised at the interesting effects you can achieve.

▶ HOW TO DO IT

Activate any layer (other than the background layer) with image data on it—this could be a photo, some painted lines, etc. Then, use the pull-down menu at the top of the layers palette to switch the mode of this layer. (For a quick start, open two photographs. Select part [or all] of one image, then copy and paste it into the other image, creating a new layer. Then, switch the modes on the copied [top] layer and watch the results.)

At the bottom of the page is an overview of the differences between modes; this is just for reference. What's important is to get a feel for the looks you can create.

On the left is the background image, and in the center is the image on the layer above it. On the right, in the Normal mode, the top layer obscures the bottom one.

In other modes (left to right: Hue, Difference, Hard Light), the top layer interacts with the bottom layer in interesting—often very appealing—ways.

OVERVIEW OF SOME INTERESTING MODES

NORMAL—No change takes place.

DISSOLVE—Pixels scatter based on their transparency.

MULTIPLY—The mathematical value of the top layer is multiplied by that of the bottom layer(s).

SCREEN—The mathematical value of the top layer is added to that of the bottom layer(s).

OVERLAY—Light areas in the top layer are "screened" (see above), dark layers are "multiplied" (see above).

SOFT LIGHT—Based on the overlying layer, treats black as burning and white as dodging.

HARD LIGHT—Very similar to the Overlay mode.

COLOR DODGE—Similar to both Screen and Lighten, tends to lighten images.

COLOR BURN—Like Color Dodge, but darkens images.

DARKEN—Chooses the darkest values of the affected pixels.

LIGHTEN—Chooses the lightest values of the affected pixels.

DIFFERENCE—Displays the difference between the top and bottom pixels based on their hue and brightness.

EXCLUSION—Inverts colors in the underlying area based on the lighter areas in the layer above.

HUE—Alters the color of the layer without affecting the brightness or saturation.

SATURATION—Saturation of the upper layer replaces that of the lower level.

COLOR—Colors of upper level replace colors of lower level, while brightness remains constant.

LUMINOSITY—Retains underlying layer's color and saturation while basing brightness on the upper layer.

LAYER OPACITY

▶ WHAT IT MEANS

A layer's opacity determines how transparent it is (or how much of the underlying layer[s] will be visible through it). When an overlying layer is somewhat transparent, it will often blend very nicely with the layers under it.

▶ HOW TO DO IT

In the layers palette, click on an overlying layer (not the background) to activate it. Then, at the top of the palette, set the opacity as you like. At 0% the layer will be invisible, at 100% it will be opaque. A sequence of examples is shown below.

Layer opacity at 100%.

Layer opacity at 75%.

Original photograph (courtesy of Rick Ferro). To create the vignette seen in this series, the following procedures were followed. First, the Elliptical Marquee was used to create an oval selection in the center of the image. Then, the selection was inversed and feathered 40 pixels. A new layer was created and the selected area was filled with black. Next, the opacity of the new layer was adjusted.

Layer opacity at 50%.

Layer opacity at 25%.

ADJUSTMENT LAYERS

▶ WHAT IT MEANS

Adjustment layers combine the features of layers with the functions of the Curves, Levels, Brightness/Contrast, Invert, and Posterize tools.

There are several advantages to using these tools on an adjustment level. First, because the effects are seen on the image but contained on a discrete level, you can toss the offending layer in the trash if it doesn't look right. Second, because the effect is on a layer, you can reduce the opacity of the layer to reduce the impact of the change—a great way to really finesse your image. Third, you can also change the layer mode of the adjustment layer to make it blend with the underlying layer in useful ways. Finally, you can access the tool's settings on this layer again and again—they don't zero out or return to the default settings when you hit OK.

▶ HOW TO DO IT

Identify the layer you want to modify by activating it in the layers palette. Go to Layer>New Adjustent Layer and select the tool you want to use. In the New Layer dialogue box (see page 87) enter the settings you want, and hit OK. Then, the dialogue box (if any) for the selected tool will open. This will work as described in the previous sections on individual tools. (Alternately, you can create new Adjustment Layer by clicking on the Adjustment Layer icon at the bottom of the layers palette and selecting the tool you want to use.)

▶ EDITING ADJUSTMENTS

In the layers palette, adjustment layers look rather unique. They contain a thumbnail image of the layer contents, like most layers, but also display a linked icon (note the chain) representing the adjustment tool used. If you want to change the values you entered for the tool, simply click on its icon in the layer. This will reopen the appropriate dialogue box so you can edit the current settings.

Adjustment layer

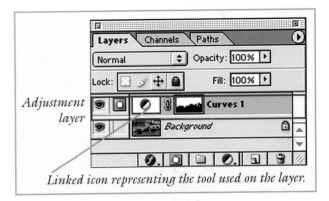

Linked icon representing the tool used on the layer.

The background of this image seemed washed out.

The background was selected and darkened using the Curves tool on an Adjustment Layer.

To make the effect a little more natural looking, the opacity of the Adjustment Layer was set to 70%.

LAYER STYLES

▶ WHAT IT MEANS

Sometimes you don't want your layers to blend seamlessly with each other—you may even want them to look very much separate. The layer styles will help you create visual definition and add a sense of depth.

▶ HOW TO DO IT

Begin with an image that has two (or more) layers. In the example below, the background layer is white, then a new layer was created and a circle selected on it using the Marquee tool. Using the Fill command, the circle was then made blue. As shown here, the image data on the layer where you create the effect should have some free edges (not fill the entire layer edge to edge).

Go to Layer>Layer Style and select an option from the list. (Skip Blending Options for now—come back to it when you feel like experimenting.) After you select an option, a layer styles dialogue box will appear. The box for each effect is slightly different, but the basic features are the same—and a little experimenting will make them clear, since the effects are instantly previewed. Generally, the layer styles dialogue box will allow you to control:

Blend Mode—Same as the layer modes discussed on page 89.
Accent Color—Click on the color box to the right of the Blend Mode menu to open the color picker.

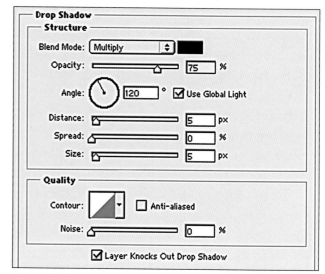

Drop shadow settings from the layer styles dialogue box.

Angle—Angle from which light seems to hit the new texture (choose Use Global Angle, and this will remain constant for all styles applied to the image, creating a more realistic look).
Distance—How many pixels in or out from the edge are affected.
Spread, Size—Basically controls how soft or hard the effect looks.
Contour—Allows you to choose an edge texture from the preset list.
Anti-Aliased—When active, softens the edges and prevents them from looking jagged.
Noise—Controls how speckled the edge of the shadow will look.
Layer Knocks Out Drop Shadow—Prevents the shadow from showing through any transparent parts of the layer.

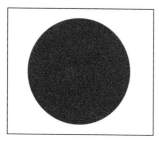

No layer style applied.

Bevel & Emboss applied.

Drop Shadow applied.

Inner Shadow applied.

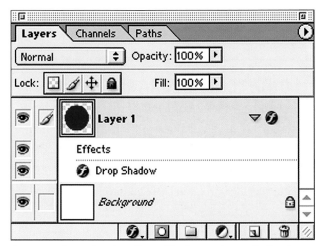

Layers palette showing Drop Shadow style applied to layer.

▶ IN THE LAYERS PALETTE

When you have applied a style, it will appear as a new layer directly below the layer to which it was applied. These layers are considered "nested," meaning the layer style will follow the original layer if you move it or delete it. You can, however, delete the style layer *without* deleting the original layer; simply drag the style layer into the trash can at the bottom of the palette. If you have a lot of layers with styles applied, the layers palette can become hard to navigate. To simplify, click on the downward-pointing arrow near the layer style icon (the black circle) near the edge of the layer to which you applied the style. This will hide the nested layer. Click it again to reexpose the layer.

▶ EDITING LAYER STYLES

If you decide you want to modify a layer style, you can access its dialogue box directly from the layer. Simply double click on the name of the effect in the style layer (in the example to the left, you'd click on "Drop Shadow").

> **QUICK TIP**
>
> Layer styles cannot be applied to the background layer. To apply a style to this material, duplicate the background layer and apply the style to the copy.

MERGING/FLATTENING LAYERS

▶ WHAT IT MEANS

For several reasons, you may eventually need to get rid of the layers in your image. As previously noted, multiple layers make an image take up more space on your hard drive require and more memory to load and/or edit. This can be a problem if, for example, you want an image to open quickly on your web page. Also, most file formats (see page 11) do not support layers—they just don't speak that "language" (in fact, only the Photoshop and TIF formats do allow them). If you plan to use your file in a program that requires specific file formats and none of these accommodate layers, you'll need to get rid of your layers. Also, you may just find that having a lot of layers makes it confusing to navigate in your layers palette. In this case, you might want to get rid of the layers you have finished, but preserve the layers you still want to work on.

▶ FLATTENING

To get rid of all of your layers while preserving the data on them, go to Layer>Flatten Image. This will composite all of the layers down into one—preserving all of the effects, opacity settings, etc., you've added.

▶ MERGE DOWN

To composite a layer with the one directly below it, select the layer to be composited, then go to Layer>Merge Down.

▶ MERGE VISIBLE

To composite some (not all) of your layers, make invisible (see page 88) the ones you want to preserve. Then, click on a visible layer to activate it and go to Layer>Merge Visible.

SAVING FILES WITH LAYERS

▶ WHAT IT MEANS

As you can probably tell already, layers allow you to edit your images in ways that traditional artists—like painters—can only dream of. Because digital images are so malleable (and digital artists so very creative), you may often find that you want to return to an image several times to make changes, improvements, or variations.

For this reason, it's a good idea to save an archival, working copy of your image *before* you do any flattening or merging of layers. By preserving all the layers, you will preserve the widest range of future editing options. You may wish to save these working images in a separate file on your hard drive, or tag them with a character or letter sequence to identify them quickly. (I place an exclamation point [!] in front of the file name to indicate an archival file or a work in progress, but you could just as easily use "arch_[filename]"—or whatever you like.)

▶ HOW TO DO IT

To save your file with the layers intact, before doing any flattening or merging of layers, go to

LONG-TERM STORAGE

Sadly, image files require lots of space to store, and most of us have a finite budget to spend on hard drives. Even more sadly, hard drives aren't perfect—on (thankfully) rare occasions, they crash quite spectacularly and chew up huge chunks of our precious data when they go. For both of these reasons, it makes sense to find additional means of storing and protecting images. While the ideal solution varies from person to person, using a CD/DVD burner to save images on a disc is a popular choice. CDs are very cheap and hold a lot of data; DVDs are more expensive but hold a lot more. Once burned, these discs are easy to access and catalog—and, in the case of CD-Rs, they make it impossible to accidentally delete your data. Because of these benefits, if you're serious about digital imaging, you should make sure that a CD/DVD burner is part of your workstation.

File>Save As. Then, select the Photoshop file format from the pull-down menu, name your image, and hit OK.

An archival copy of each image should be saved in case you decide to make future revisions. Here, the archival file (!venice 10.psd) was saved with its twelve layers preserved; it requires 81.4MB to store. Its flattened counterpart (venice 10/final.tif) requires only 6.2MB. (Normally, you won't need to use or save this many layers, so the disparity in memory size usually won't be quite this dramatic.) The archival file is stored in the Photoshop (.psd) format, which is ideal for saving layers. The final file is saved in the TIF format (.tif), because this is portable to a wide range of other applications. If this photo was to be used on a web page, you might save still another copy that was compressed (see page 11) and optimized for the Internet. Finally, the original, unaltered image is saved and labeled as an original. This is especially important if you shot it with a digital camera, since you don't have a negative to go back to if something should happen to your finished file—call it a cheap insurance policy.

USING THE
HISTORY PALETTE

IMPORTANT TERMS

History State—A point in the history of an image. This point is preserved as long as the number of history states does not exceed your set maximum.

Snapshot—A point in the history of an image that is preserved regardless of the number of states in the total history.

THE HISTORY PALETTE

▶ WHAT IT MEANS

The history palette is a relatively recent addition to Photoshop—and one you'll be happy you don't have to live without. Up to this point, when you've wanted to undo something you've used the Edit>Undo command. Unfortunately, this can only undo the very last thing you did. So what happens if you realize you made a terrible mistake three steps back? Well, it used to be that you'd have to start over from scratch. As you can imagine, this was a pretty frustrating situation.

The addition of the history palette changed all that, by creating a permanent timeline of each step executed by the user (that's you). By accessing the states (individual steps) in this timeline, you can move back and forth through the history of the image and compare previous versions to the current one, or to undo the last ten steps, during which—in a misguided attempt at humor—you painted clown makeup on your grandmother's bridal portrait.

▶ HISTORY PALETTE

If the history palette is not visible on your desktop, go to Window>History. If you have an image open on which you've performed some operations, your palette will look something like the one shown below. If you have just opened an image, your palette will not have any stages (other than Open) shown beyond the initial snapshot.

▶ HISTORY PREFERENCES

Photoshop's default setting is to store only twenty history states. If you exceed that maximum while working on an image, the earliest states will automatically be removed to make room for the new ones. You may wish to increase the number of stages it remembers. To do this, go to Edit> Preferences>General and increase the History States setting. Forty or fifty will likely be sufficient for nearly every editing session you do. Storing the history states (essentially multiple copies of the image) requires lots of your computer's memory, so try not to select an excessive setting.

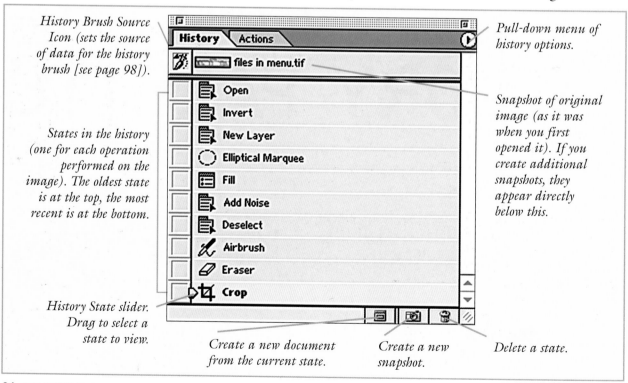

History Brush Source Icon (sets the source of data for the history brush [see page 98]).

States in the history (one for each operation performed on the image). The oldest state is at the top, the most recent is at the bottom.

History State slider. Drag to select a state to view.

Pull-down menu of history options.

Snapshot of original image (as it was when you first opened it). If you create additional snapshots, they appear directly below this.

Create a new document from the current state.

Create a new snapshot.

Delete a state.

▶ HOW TO DO IT

To get started, open an image and perform a few operations—crop it, paint on it, adjust the curves, whatever. As you do so, keep an eye on the history palette. You should notice that, as you perform each operation, a new stage (bearing a descriptive name) is added to the list.

To move back in time, click on the stage you want to go back to (click on the name of the state or the icon next to it). Alternately, you can drag the History State slider up or down to the state you want to see. You can move up and down the list as many times as you want.

▶ STRATEGIES

Simple Backtrack—As you move backwards chronologically in the states (i.e., up the list), the states below the active one (those more recent than the state you are viewing) will be grayed out. If you want to abandon (delete) these states, just begin working again from the earlier state.

Try a New Direction (Without Abandoning the Old One)—Sometimes, you will reach a point in your work where you like what you've done, but you have a couple of ideas you want to try out to finish the job. In these cases, try hitting the icon at the bottom of the history palette (see page 96) that creates a new document from the current state. This will instantly create an identical image in a new window. You can then try out one idea on the original image and the other idea on the new image.

"Bookmark" a State—As you're working on an image, you may reach a point where you want to keep a record of the way something looked in the current version, or to create a permanent shortcut to a particular state. To do this, simply select the state from the history palette and click on the icon at the bottom of the palette (see page 96) to create a new snapshot. This snapshot will be added at the top of the history palette directly under the snapshot of the original image. You can add as many snapshots as you like.

Step 1: *After adjusting the curves and converting the image to the CMYK color mode, the image was colorized by going to Hue/ Saturation (see pages 46–47). (Original photograph courtesy of Jeff Smith.)*

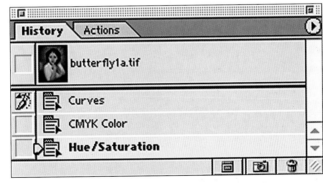 

Step 2: *Although the sepia tone looked nice, the original color version seemed better. To reverse the process, just click on the previous state in the palette (in this case, "CMYK Color"). The conversion to CMYK could also have been undone by clicking on the step above it ("Curves").*

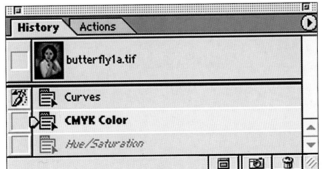 

HISTORY BRUSH

▶ WHAT IT IS

The History Brush is like the best kind of time machine. With it, you can pick and choose just those parts of your image's history that you like. In essence, it allows you to selectively paint the pretty parts of its history back onto the image.

▶ HOW TO DO IT

Select a previous state from the history palette and activate the History Brush Source icon at that level. Then, select the History Brush from the toolbar (see page 50). Choose a brush and proceed to use the tool exactly as you would the Brush tool (see page 77). Options for the History Brush are the same as those for the Brush tool. For the most seamless effect, select a soft brush.

▶ ART HISTORY BRUSH

A variation on the History Brush, this tool allows you to paint with simulated brush-stroke patterns. To use it, select a previous state from the history palette and activate the History Brush Source icon at that level. Select the Art History Brush from the toolbar (see page 50), then choose a brush. Select a Style (type of stroke), Fidelity (accuracy of rendition) and Area (size of coverage), and begin painting. The effect can be quite realistic with a small brush, or very abstract with a large one.

Step 1: *The image is opened. (Original photograph courtesy of Jeff Smith.)*

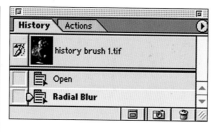

Step 2: *The Radial Blur filter is applied (Filter>Blur>Radial Blur).*

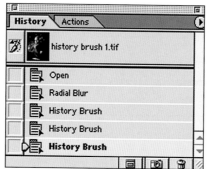

Step 3: *The History Brush Source icon was placed next to the original image snapshot. Then, the History Brush was selected. With a soft brush, data from the original image was painted onto the blurred one. This selectively restored the original appearance of the subject's face and hand.*

MAKING TRANSFORMATIONS

IMPORTANT TERMS

Distort—To change the overall shape of a selected area of image data.

Flip—To reverse a selected area of image data, either top to bottom (vertically) or left to right (horizontally).

Rotate—To turn a selected area of image data around a fixed point.

Scale—To change the size of a selected area of image data.

SCALE

▶ WHAT IT MEANS

Scaling is one of the many features by which you can transform the size and shape of image data on a layer. Scaling allows you to increase or decrease the height and/or width of the image.

▶ HOW TO DO IT

To practice, open an image and select an area of it with the Marquee tool (see page 54). Copy this area (Edit>Copy) and paste it (Edit>Paste). This will duplicate the selected data on a new layer. Then, go to Edit>Transform>Scale. Doing this will cause a rectangular box to appear around the image data on your new layer. At each corner you'll find a small box (called a handle). Hold down the Shift key, then click on a corner handle and drag it to scale the image. Click on any handle and drag it to stretch or compress the image.

Hit Return to accept the change, or select another function from the transform menu to further adjust your image.

▶ IMPORTANT NOTES

Transform functions cannot be used on the background layer unless it contains an active selection. Then, the selected area will be transformed.

Original image.   *Image being scaled.*

ROTATE

▶ WHAT IT MEANS

Rotating allows you to turn an image to any angle you choose.

▶ HOW TO DO IT

To practice, open an image and use the Marquee tool (see page 54) to select an area of it. Copy this area (Edit>Copy) and then paste it (Edit>Paste). Then, go to Edit>Transform>Rotate. Doing this will cause a rectangular box with handles to appear around the image data on your new layer. Click on any handle and drag it around the perimeter of the rectangle to rotate the image.

Hit Return to accept the change, or select another function from the transform menu to further change your image.

▶ IMPORTANT NOTES

With the transform functions, it's okay if you drag the handles out of the visible image area. If you need to access a handle you can't see, simply reduce the image view using the percentage view or Zoom tool (see page 15) until you can see the handle you want to move.

Original image.   *Image being rotated.*

SKEW AND DISTORT

▶ WHAT IT MEANS

The Skew and Distort function are very similar, and allow you to move one (or more) corners/ sides of an image to warp the image in interesting ways.

▶ SKEW: HOW TO DO IT

To practice, open an image and use the Marquee tool (see page 54) to select an area of it. Copy this area (Edit>Copy) and paste it (Edit>Paste). Then, go to Edit>Transform>Skew. Doing this will cause a rectangular box with handles to appear around the image data on your new layer. Click on any handle and drag it to skew the image. The handles will move only in a straight line in a given direction.

▶ DISTORT: HOW TO DO IT

To practice, open an image and use the Marquee tool (see page 54) to select an area of it. Copy this area (Edit>Copy) and paste it (Edit>Paste). Then, go to Edit>Transform> Distort. Doing this will cause a rectangular box with handles to appear around the image data on your new layer. Click on any handle and drag it to distort the image. The handles will move freely in every direction.

With either tool, hit Return to accept the change, or select another function from the Transform menu to further adjust your image.

Skewed image.

Distorted image.

TIPS

REPEAT—To repeat the previous transformation, go to Edit>Transform>Again.

LINKS—If the layer on which you perform a transformation in linked to any other layers (see page 88), those layers will also undergo the same transformation.

PERSPECTIVE

▶ WHAT IT MEANS

The Perspective feature allows you to add the appearance of distance to your image.

▶ HOW TO DO IT

To practice, open an image and use the Marquee tool (see page 54) to select an area of it. Copy this area (Edit>Copy) and paste it (Edit>Paste). Activate the new layer in the layers palette, then go to Edit>Transform> Perspective. This will cause a box with handles to appear around the data on the new layer. Click on any corner handle. Drag it toward the center of the image to make that area seem to recede into the background (or drag it away from

Original image.

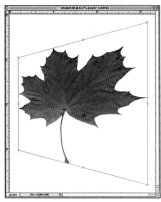

Transforming perspective.

the center to make that area seem to pop out). Hit Return to accept the change, or select another function from the transform menu.

ROTATE AND FLIP

▶ WHAT IT MEANS

The Rotate and Flip features allow you to re-orient your image in five preset ways.

▶ HOW TO DO IT

To practice, open an image and use the Marquee tool (see page 54) to select an area of it. Copy this area (Edit>Copy) and paste it (Edit>Paste). Activate the new layer in the layers palette, then go to Edit>Transform and select Rotate 180°, Rotate 90° CW (clockwise), Rotate 90° CCW (counterclockwise), Flip Horizontal (left to right) or Flip Vertical (top to bottom). The change will be applied instantly.

Original image.

Rotated 180°.

OTHER
USEFUL GOODIES

IMPORTANT TERMS

Action—A predetermined or user-determined sequence of operations that can be performed automatically on demand.

Batch Process—Automated process by which a user can automatically apply an action to an entire group of images.

Droplet—A free-standing application that performs the steps of an action.

Revert—To return to a previously saved version of an image or to an earlier state of that image.

LIQUIFY

▶ WHAT IT MEANS

The Liquify command allows you to freely twist, stretch, and warp an image.

▶ HOW TO DO IT

Go to Filter>Liquify. Doing so will open a full-screen dialogue box with a large preview of your image in the center and two control panels on either side. To the left of your image are the liquify tools (see below), and to the right are the liquify options (see below).

Next, select one of the liquify tools—begin with either the Warp, Twist, Pucker, Bloat, Shift Pixels, or Reflection tools. Once you've made your selection, choose a brush from the options panel to the right of your image preview. For the most impact, select a rather large brush (perhaps in the 50–100 range), and set the brush pressure to about 50 (higher settings will provide even more distortion). Then, by clicking and dragging over the image preview, simply begin painting on the distortion. The longer you leave your brush in one

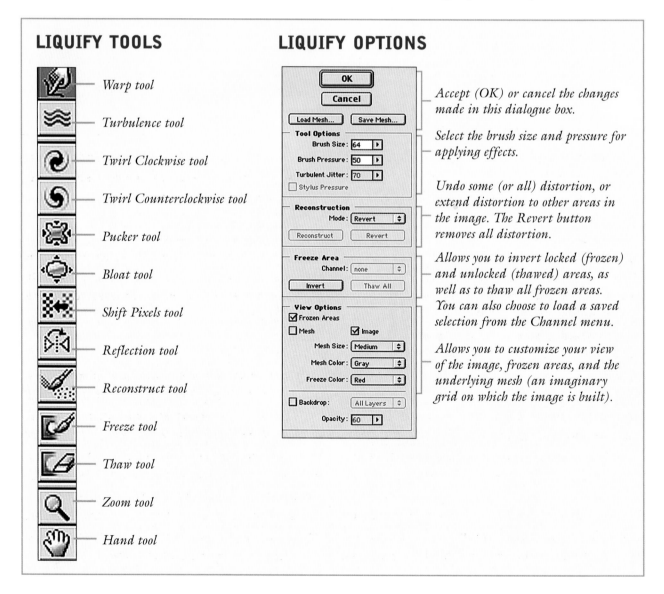

LIQUIFY TOOLS

— Warp tool

— Turbulence tool

— Twirl Clockwise tool

— Twirl Counterclockwise tool

— Pucker tool

— Bloat tool

— Shift Pixels tool

— Reflection tool

— Reconstruct tool

— Freeze tool

— Thaw tool

— Zoom tool

— Hand tool

LIQUIFY OPTIONS

OK

Cancel

Load Mesh...   Save Mesh...

Tool Options
Brush Size: 64
Brush Pressure: 50
Turbulent Jitter: 70
☐ Stylus Pressure

Reconstruction
Mode: Revert
Reconstruct   Revert

Freeze Area
Channel: none
Invert   Thaw All

View Options
☑ Frozen Areas
☐ Mesh   ☑ Image
Mesh Size: Medium
Mesh Color: Gray
Freeze Color: Red
☐ Backdrop: All Layers
Opacity: 60

Accept (OK) or cancel the changes made in this dialogue box.

Select the brush size and pressure for applying effects.

Undo some (or all) distortion, or extend distortion to other areas in the image. The Revert button removes all distortion.

Allows you to invert locked (frozen) and unlocked (thawed) areas, as well as to thaw all frozen areas. You can also choose to load a saved selection from the Channel menu.

Allows you to customize your view of the image, frozen areas, and the underlying mesh (an imaginary grid on which the image is built).

Above: *Original image.*
Right: *Image with distortion effects applied using the Liquify command.*

area, the more the pixels there will be distorted. Try experimenting with several of the aforementioned tools using different brush sizes and pressures, and painting quickly versus slowly.

▶ FREEZE/THAW

If you don't want to distort (or further distort) part of your image, use the freeze tool to lock that area. Simply select the tool, choose a brush, and paint over the area you want to freeze. (In View Options at the bottom of the options panel, make sure Frozen Areas is checked. You can select a Freeze Color from the pull-down menu at the bottom of this panel, as well—this is the color used to indicate an area is frozen.) To thaw (unlock) an area, select the Thaw tool, choose a brush, and paint over the area you want to unlock.

To make a frozen area conform to a selection, before choosing the liquify command, make and save a selection (see page 66). Deactivate the

selection, then go to Filter>Liquify. Under Freeze Area in the options panel, choose your saved selection from the pull-down menu.

▶ REVERT

If you like the results, hit OK to accept the changes. If you don't like them but you want to try again, hit Revert under the reconstruction section of the options panel.

▶ RECONSTRUCTION

To reconstruct the entire image (which takes it back toward its original state, but usually not all the way), hit the Reconstruct button. To *selectively undo* distortion, choose the Reconstruct tool from the toolbar. Then, select a brush and pressure. In the Reconstruction area of the options menu, you'll find a pull-down menu of reconstruction modes. Each of these reconstructs the image in a slightly different way—experiment to see which one best suits your purpose.

ACTIONS

▶ WHAT IT MEANS

Actions are the robotic helpmate of the Photoshop user. While no action is smart or creative enough to accomplish anything unique, actions can quickly execute a pre- or user-determined sequence of tasks. This means, when very repetitive jobs need to be done (say, converting a hundred images to 72dpi and RGB for use on your web site), you only need to hit one button to perform both functions in sequence.

▶ HOW TO DO IT

Conveniently, Photoshop comes packaged with a number of preset actions that work very well. These appear in the actions palette (see below). If your actions palette lists only the default set of actions, go to the pull-down menu at the top right corner of the actions palette and select the other available sets from the bottom of the list (these are the entries that end in ".atn"—the marker for an actions file format).

To try out the preset actions, begin by opening an image. Select an action from the actions palette by clicking on the action's name. (*Note:* Some actions can only be performed on specific types of data, like text [see page 112], a selection, or a layer. This is noted in parentheses after the name of the action. You must fulfill this prerequisite for the action to work.)

Once you have selected an action, review its Toggle Dialogue setting. If it's active, Photoshop will pause at each dialogue box for you to enter settings. If it's inactive, the predetermined settings will be used. For now, uncheck this box by clicking on it until the dialogue box icon disappears. Then, to engage the action, hit the play button at the bottom of the actions palette; Photoshop will do the rest. When the action has finished playing, you may want to switch to the history palette and look at all of the steps it enacted while playing.

▶ CUSTOM ACTIONS

Photoshop also allows you to create your own actions for things that you personally find you do again and again. Maybe you convert a lot of images to grayscale, or perhaps you like a particular combination of filters. With actions you can apply these at the touch of a button. Here's how to record an action of your own:

1. Open an image.

2. Go to the actions palette and click the Create New Set icon at the bottom of the palette. Then, name the set "custom set" (or whatever you like) in the dialogue box that appears.

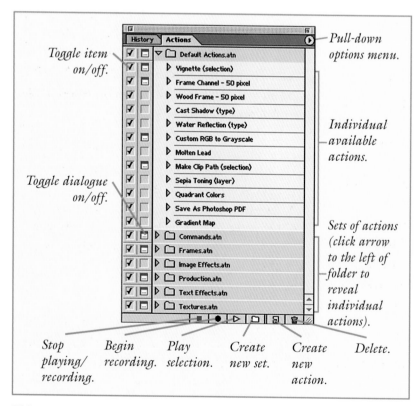

Toggle item on/off.

Toggle dialogue on/off.

Pull-down options menu.

Individual available actions.

Sets of actions (click arrow to the left of folder to reveal individual actions).

Stop playing/ recording.

Begin recording.

Play selection.

Create new set.

Create new action.

Delete.

Original image.

Ripple Frame (preset action).

Aged Photo (preset action).

Original text.

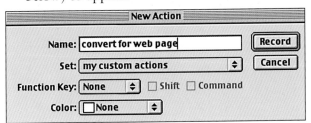

Brushed Metal (preset action).

Sprayed Stencil (preset action).

3. Go to the pull-down menu at the top right corner of the actions palette and select New Action. This will cause a dialogue box (see below) to appear.

> **New Action**
>
> Name: convert for web page   Record
> Set: my custom actions   Cancel
> Function Key: None ☐ Shift ☐ Command
> Color: ☐ None

In this box, name your new action, then select the newly created "custom set" folder. If you like, you can also select a function key (a shortcut to the action) and a highlight color for the action as it appears in the list of actions.

4. Hit Record, then carefully perform the steps you want to be included in the action—changing the resolution, running a filter, etc. (*Note:* A few functions, such as Brush tool strokes and cropping, cannot be recorded in the actions. For this reason, it's a good idea to test your action on a duplicate image before putting it to work.)

5. When you have finished, hit the Stop button at the bottom of the actions palette.

To apply your new action, simply follow the directions given on the previous page ("How to Do It").

DROPLETS

Photoshop can turn an action into its own application, called a droplet. This can sit on your desktop or in a folder, or be shared with other Photoshop users. If you drag a file (or folder of files) onto the droplet icon, Photoshop will launch (if it's not already open) and the action will be executed. Here's how to make a droplet:

Droplet icon.

1. Go to File>Automate>Create Droplet.
2. Click Choose and select the location where you want to save the droplet.
3. Choose an action set and a specific action.
4. Choose destination options (these are very similar to those for batch processing—refer to page 108 for elaboration).
5. Hit OK.

To use a Macintosh droplet on a PC, add **.exe** to the file name. To use a PC droplet on a Mac, drag the droplet onto the Photoshop application icon.

BATCH PROCESSING

▶ WHAT IT MEANS

Batch processing puts actions to heavy-duty work by allowing you to automatically apply an action to a group of images. The batch-process function will open the images, perform your specified action, then save them in a folder you specify—all while you enjoy a cup of coffee or catch up on your reading.

▶ HOW TO DO IT

To begin, place all the images you want to process together in one folder. Then, go to File> Automate>Batch. A window like the one shown below will open up. From the Play section, specify the action to be applied by selecting the desired action from its set. From Source, select Folder, then hit Choose and identify the folder that contains the images you want to process. (Additional options are listed below but will normally not be needed.) Under Destination, select Folder, then hit Choose and identify the specific folder where you want the processed images to be stored (or create a new folder to house them). Under File Naming, you can rename your processed files using the pull-down menus, or leave them as is by selecting the default settings shown below. When the settings seem right, hit OK and watch your computer go to work. This can be a little confusing at first, so you may want to practice with a duplicate set of images.

TIPS

You can also set the destination to Save and Close. This will save the processed image over the original without switching folders. (Note: This means your original image will be permanently replaced.) For safety, you should create a duplicate set of backup originals before using this option.

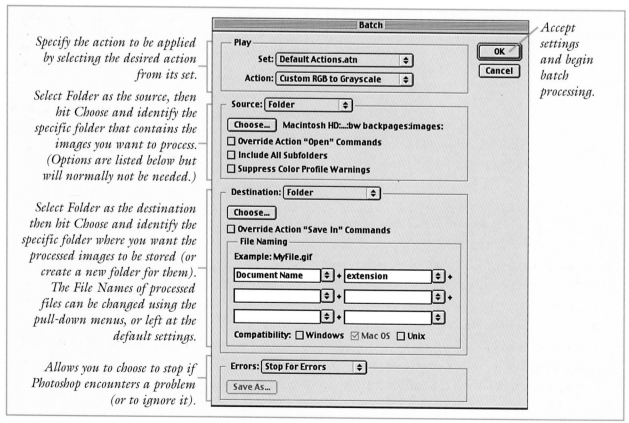

Specify the action to be applied by selecting the desired action from its set.

Select Folder as the source, then hit Choose and identify the specific folder that contains the images you want to process. (Options are listed below but will normally not be needed.)

Select Folder as the destination then hit Choose and identify the specific folder where you want the processed images to be stored (or create a new folder for them). The File Names of processed files can be changed using the pull-down menus, or left at the default settings.

Allows you to choose to stop if Photoshop encounters a problem (or to ignore it).

Accept settings and begin batch processing.

ADDING TEXT

IMPORTANT TERMS

Anti-Aliasing—Function that helps to smooth the edges of curves and prevent jagged edges.

Mask—Indication of a selection. Instead of using dotted lines to surround the selection, the *unselected* area is covered by transparent red, indicating that this area cannot be altered.

Rasterize—Some artwork (such as text) is made up of lines drawn according to mathematical equations. Rasterizing causes these lines to be converted into dots (pixels).

Warp—Feature that allows you to bend and twist text.

NEW TEXT

▶ WHAT IT MEANS

Using the Text tool, you can added lettering in almost any imaginable shape or form to your Photoshop images.

▶ HOW TO DO IT

Select the Text tool from the toolbar (see page 50), then set the options palette as you like. Click anywhere on your image and a blinking cursor will appear. From here, begin typing your text. When you have finished, click the "⊘" to cancel your work (cancel current edits) or the "✓" button to accept it (commit current edits). Selecting a new tool will automatically commit the current edits. Every time you use the Text tool, a new layer will be created for the text, so you can always delete or edit the text if you are unhappy with the effect.

▶ OPTIONS

Just as you would in a word-processing program, you have a number of options for fine-tuning your text. Accessed via the options palette (see below), these are (from left to right):

Change the Text Orientation—Allows you to toggle between text that runs across the page or up and down it.

Font—From the pull-down menu, select the style of type (font) you wish to use from those installed on your computer.

Font Style—From the pull-down menu, choose regular or another style (the styles available vary from font to font).

Font Size—Select a size from the pull-down list, or type in your own value.

Anti-Aliasing Method—This determines how smooth the curves on your text will look (leave this set to Crisp unless there is a specific reason to change it).

Paragraph Justification—Controls how the lines in a paragraph are aligned (flush left, centered, or flush right).

Text Color—Sets the color of the text. Click on this box to activate the Color Picker (see page 75), then select a color.

As you continue across the options palette, you'll encounter a few options that, when accessed, open up their own dialogue boxes.

▶ TEXT WARP

This feature allows you to bend and twist your text. In the text options palette, access the dialogue box (see top of the facing page) for this feature by clicking the "T" icon with the bent line under it. Simply select the style of warp you want, then choose a vertical or horizontal warp. By adjusting the bend, horizontal distortion, and vertical distortion, you can set the warp as you like.

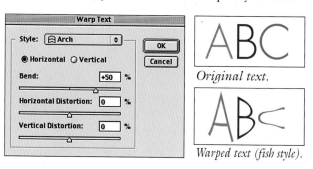

Original text.

Warped text (fish style).

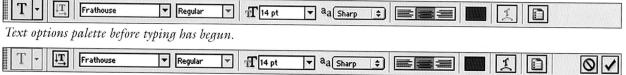

Text options palette before typing has begun.

Text options palette after typing has begun. At the far right, the "⊘" (cancel current edits) and "✓" (commit current edits) buttons are added.

▶ CHARACTER PALETTE

The character palette offers some of the same controls as seen on the regular text options palette, but supplements them with additional features. Kerning (the ability to change the space between two letters), vertical/horizontal scaling, and baseline shifts are all controlled from this panel. You can also select to change your text to all caps, to super- or subscript it, to underline it, and more.

▶ PARAGRAPH PALETTE

The paragraph palette also duplicates some of the same controls as seen on the options palette. Added features include the ability to set indents, to insert spaces before or after each paragraph, and to allow automatic hyphenation.

▶ EDITING TEXT

To edit your text, activate the layer containing the text in the layers palette. Then, select the text tool and click on the text to reactivate the cursor. You can also select strings of text by clicking and dragging over the letters (this allows you to change the font, size, etc., of those letters). You can also cut/copy and paste text by selecting it and going to Edit>Cut (or Copy) and Edit>Paste.

CHARACTER PALETTE

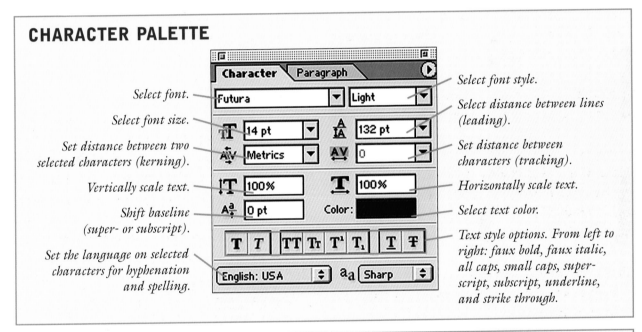

Select font. — Futura / Light — Select font style.

Select font size. — T 14 pt — Select distance between lines (leading). / 132 pt

Set distance between two selected characters (kerning). — AV Metrics / AV 0 — Set distance between characters (tracking).

Vertically scale text. — T 100% / T 100% — Horizontally scale text.

Shift baseline (super- or subscript). — Aª 0 pt / Color: — Select text color.

Set the language on selected characters for hyphenation and spelling. — English: USA / aa Sharp — Text style options. From left to right: faux bold, faux italic, all caps, small caps, superscript, subscript, underline, and strike through.

PARAGRAPH PALETTE

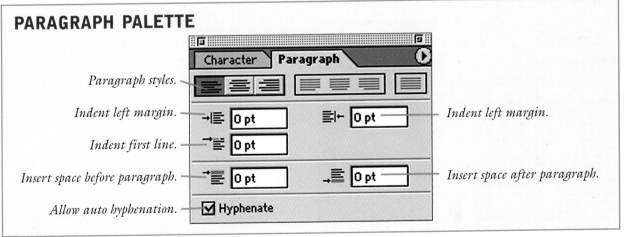

Paragraph styles. — [Character / Paragraph]

Indent left margin. — 0 pt / 0 pt — Indent left margin.

Indent first line. — 0 pt

Insert space before paragraph. — 0 pt / 0 pt — Insert space after paragraph.

Allow auto hyphenation. — ☑ Hyphenate

TEXT EFFECTS

▶ WHAT IT MEANS

Photoshop allows you to do weird and wonderful things with text—things your word processor never dreamed of! Step-by-step instructions for several interesting techniques are provided in this section. These are, however, just a starting point; you should certainly experiment with your own variations or unique ideas!

▶ ADDING LAYER EFFECTS

When you create your text, it forms on a new layer. That means you can use the layers features to spice up your text. For example, you can change the layer mode or opacity (see pages 89–90).

Plain text (photo courtesy of Jeff Hawkins). *Text layer set to the overlay mode.*

You can also use the layer styles (see pages 92–93), provided that you first rasterize your text. (Text is created as what is called "vector" art, meaning it is made up of lines drawn according to mathematical equations. Rasterizing the text turns it into pixels [dots] like the other data in the image. Once text is rasterized, however, it can no longer be edited.) To rasterize your text, activate the layer it is on in the layers palette, then go to Layer>Rasterize>

Plain text (photo courtesy of Jeff Hawkins). *Rasterized text layer with Outer Glow layer style.*

Type. One effect that is commonly added to text is a drop shadow. This can be done by rasterizing the text, choosing the text layer from the layers palette and applying the Drop Shadow layer style (Layer>Layer Style>Drop Shadow).

Plain text.

Rasterized text layer with drop shadow layer style.

▶ ACTIONS FOR TEXT

As noted on page 106, Photoshop is equipped with a number of interesting actions that can change the appearance of your text. To use them, look for actions that say "(text)" after their description. Activate your text layer in the layers palette and run the action (see pages 106–7 for instructions on running actions).

Plain text. *Die Cut action.*

 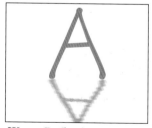

Running Water action. *Water Reflection action.*

You can expand your creativity with text by working with it as a selection. Here's how to do it:

1. Add your text to the image (see pages 110–11).

2. Rasterize the text (Layer>Rasterize>Text).

3. With the layer containing the text still active in the layers palette, select the Magic Wand tool. In the options palette, set the Tolerance to 1 and make sure the Contiguous box is *not* checked. Then, click with the Magic Wand tool anywhere outside of the text.

4. Inverse the selection to choose the text (Select> Inverse) and hit Delete to clear it.

5. Just to be safe, save your selection (see page 66).

6. In the layers palette, activate the image layer (or a duplicate of it) and begin experimenting.

With the selection active and in place over your photographic image, you can run filters, adjust the Brightness/Contrast, Posterize, Invert the image, etc.—anything you might do to a photograph. Some examples are shown here.

Photo with a text selection active (photo courtesy of Jeff Hawkins).

Five-point stroke (in white) applied to selection, five-point Gaussian Blur applied within selected area.

Fresco filter applied. Then, selected area copied and pasted to new layer where Outer Glow layer style was added.

Noise filter applied. Smudge tool used to create streaks. Selected area pasted to new layer. Bevel layer style added.

When you employ the full range of tools offered by Photoshop, there's no limit to the effects you can create with your text. Two possibilities are shown below.

▶ PEBBLES

1. Begin with an image in the RGB color mode.

2. Select the Text tool and create the desired text, setting its color to a bluish gray. Click the "✓" button to accept the text.

3. Rasterize the text (Layer>Rasterize>Type).

4. Set the foreground color to black, and apply the Stained Glass filter (Filter>Texture>Stained Glass). (The foreground color determines the color of the border between the stained glass cells, so it is important that it contrast sharply with the color of the text.)

5. Using the Magic Wand (with the Contiguous setting deactivated in the options palette), select the black border between the stained glass cells. Go to (Edit>Clear) to clear the selected black area.

6. Inverse the selection (Select>Inverse) and feather it 3 pixels. Then, deactivate the selection.

7. Apply the Bevel and Emboss layer style, followed by the Drop Shadow layer style.

▶ PLASTIC CUTOUTS

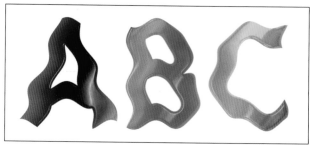

1. Begin with an image in the RGB color mode.

2. Create a new, empty layer and activate it in the layers palette.

3. Select the text tool and type your text. In the options palette, click the "✓" button to accept it.

4. Follow steps 2–4 on page 113 for turning your text into a selection.

5. With the selection active, select the Gradient tool, choose a gradient you like, and apply it to the selection (see page 81).

6. Deactivate the selection.

7. Apply the Wave filter (Filter>Distort>Wave), then apply the Plastic Wrap filter (Filter>Artistic>Plastic Wrap).

TIPS

Although Photoshop offers numerous text controls, it does not take the place of a word processor or layout software (such as QuarkXPress™ or Adobe® InDesign®). Photoshop is better used for special text effects that can't be achieved in these programs (like warping text).

PUTTING IT
ALL TOGETHER

MOVING FORWARD . . .

At this point, you have the basic skills needed to tackle just about any Photoshop job. They key is to learn how to use these tools in concert with each other. To do this, you need to develop a strategy for each project you undertake. In the beginning, this will probably take some trial and error. This is simply part of the creative process—so try not to get frustrated. As you proceed, the interplay of tools will increasingly become second nature.

The step-by-step examples in the following section explore three common types of imaging tasks: retouching a problem photograph, compositing (combining) two photos, and adding special effects to an image. As you read through these examples (or better yet, work through them with your own images), you'll begin to see the strategy that comes into play when digitally manipulating your images.

EXAMPLE 1: COMBINING TOOLS TO IMPROVE A PROBLEM IMAGE

▶ WHAT IT MEANS

Very few images can be fixed with only one tool. Usually several tools are needed. This section shows how a damaged image was restored.

▶ HOW TO DO IT

After scanning the print, a quick visual analysis was conducted and a to-do list developed. This list included the following points:

1. There were several spots and specks on the photo—as well as a few areas where the surface had torn away.
2. The photo was faded and yellowed. It had also lost some contrast.
3. The blue ink had also faded, making the inscription difficult to read.

Original image.

▶ STEP ONE: CLONE TOOL

The first step was to correct the damaged areas and the assorted spots and specks. Since these were small and scattered across the photograph, the Clone tool was used to sample nearby data and copy it over the damaged areas.

Area before correction.

Area after correction.

▶ STEP TWO: CURVES, BRIGHTNESS/CONTRAST

The next step in the restoration of this photograph was to remove the yellow color cast. This could have been accomplished using a number of different tools (Color Balance, Hue/Saturation, etc.). Since the image was in the CMYK mode, however, the yellow channel could be easily isolated and adjusted in the Curves dialogue box. Clicking at the midpoint on the line created a handle that was pulled downward to reduce the yellow in the midtones.

Before color correction.   *After color correction.*   *After contrast correction.*

▶ STEP THREE: ENHANCE TEXT

The inscription had become a little worn and faded. This was enhanced in two ways.

First, the Selective Color tool was used to increase the cyan and magenta content in the blue tones. This worked well here, since the blue ink was the only blue in the image.

However, some gaps still remained. To correct these, the Brush tool was selected and set to Wet Edges (to match the look of the ink). Using the Eyedropper tool, the ink color was selected as the foreground color. The brush size (after a couple of tries) was matched as closely as possible to the width of the ink line, and the hardness was set to about 70 to create relatively sharp edges.

Next, a new layer was created and selected in the layers palette. After zooming in tight on the inscription (using the Magnifying Glass), the letters were traced with the Brush tool set to 50% opacity. Special attention was paid to areas where gaps had developed in the original writing.

When complete, the layer was set to the Multiply layer mode, making the painted areas on the layer blend in well with the original ink underneath, and darkening the combination slightly.

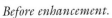

Before enhancement.   *After enhancement.*   *Final image.*

EXAMPLE 2: COMBINING TOOLS TO COMPOSITE TWO IMAGES

▶ WHAT IT MEANS

Originally, one of the most interesting uses for digital imaging software was to combine elements of two different images in a realistic way—something that is much harder to do with traditional photographic techniques. While it's no longer a primary reason to use digital imaging, compositing can still be a fun and profitable exercise.

▶ STEP ONE: IMAGE SELECTION

The criteria for selecting images to composite should be very rigorous. For realistic results, the direction and quality of lighting should be very similar in both. It helps, too, if the elements to be combined are well exposed and contain no major color problems. Also, check to make sure the focus is correct. A softly-focused subject in the midst of a sharply-focused group will not look realistic.

These images meet the lighting, exposure, and focus criteria for compositing.

Look at the images carefully and decide which one contains more of the material you want to retain in the final image. In this case, the theater will be the background. The only part of the other image that will be used is the figure in the center of the frame.

▶ STEP TWO: SELECTION OF SUBJECT

The material to be imported into the background photograph (the woman) was selected using the Lasso and Magic Wand tools—adding to and subtracting from selections as needed.

Subject is selected.

▶ STEP THREE: FEATHERING

The selection was then feathered to soften the edges and make them a little less obvious when moving the selected subject into the theater image. (Feathering the selection about 2 pixels is usually a good place to start.)

▶ STEP FOUR: COPY AND PASTE

The selected area was then copied (Edit>Copy) and pasted (Edit>Paste) into a new layer in the theater image.

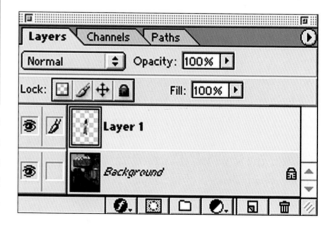

▶ STEP FIVE: POSITIONING

Once this was done, the rest of the job consisted of fine-tuning the components to make them blend as seamlessly as possible. Correct positioning of the new element on the new layer was the first task. To do this accurately, look at the scale of the imported material. Does it need to be changed in order to make sense with the subjects around it? Then, think about perspective. If your background image (as here) shows a scene in the distance, the subject must be at a correct size in relation to its apparent distance from the camera. In the images below, you can see the difference between reasonably good perspective and an obviously wrong one. In each image, the figure size remained the same; only the position changed.

Good placement.   *Bad placement.*

▶ STEP SIX: COLOR BALANCE

Next, look at the color, brightness, and contrast of the new element in relation to the background. Correct any problems using the Curves or one of the other image adjustment controls.

▶ STEP SEVEN: ADDING A SHADOW

With the image almost complete, the only thing missing was the woman's shadow. Everything else in the image has long, dark shadows; adding one to the woman enforced the realism of the effect.

To add the shadow, the layer containing the subject was duplicated in the layers palette. After activating the new layer, the Brightness/Contrast control (Image>Adjustments>Brightness/Contrast) was set to -100 on both sliders, making the subject go black on this layer.

Next, the Edit>Transform>Distort command was used to drag the top of the new layer down diag-

onally. (In this case, since the shadow needed to bend up onto a wall, a selection also needed to be made of the area of the shadow that would be on the wall. The distort function was used a second time to adjust this area.)

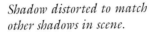

Shadow distorted to match other shadows in scene.

Top of shadow selected and distorted to run up the wall.

With the basic outline of the shadow in place, the Gaussian Blur filter (set to 5 pixels) was used to create a softer edge on the shadow. The final step was to make the shadow more transparent by reducing the opacity of the layer it was on. In this case, the opacity was set to 30%.

Final composited image.

EXAMPLE 3: COMBINING TOOLS TO ADD SPECIAL EFFECTS

▶ WHAT IT MEANS

While realistic composites are fun, sometimes it's even more fun to create something fantastic that couldn't exist in nature.

▶ HOW TO DO IT

Your imagination is the only limit when it comes to creating fantastic effects. To get started, you might like to try combining a background and an out-of-place subject, or two very different objects—you might even try to create a scene from a storybook or a dream.

In the example shown here, the image was based on a photograph of a creepy-looking, run-down hallway.

Original image.

Fog added.

Light effect added.

▶ STEP ONE: ADDING FOG

With the file in RGB, a new layer was added and activated in the layers palette. With the foreground color set to black and the background color set to white, the Clouds filter (Filter>Render>Clouds) was applied to this layer. In the history palette, the new state (Clouds) was selected as the source for the history brush. The layer was then selected (Select>All) and cleared (Edit>Clear). With the history brush set to 70% opacity, the clouds were selectively painted back onto the layer (see above) to create the look of low-lying fog. The image was then flattened.

▶ STEP TWO: LIGHT EFFECT

To enhance the sense of mystery, the Lighting Effects filter was used (Filter>Render>Lighting Effects). The style was set to Blue Omni.

▶ STEP THREE: ADD FIGURE

The figure added to the photo was simply borrowed from a photo of a woman in a dress. The woman was selected from the photo using the lasso tool. The selection was then feathered two pixels. After reducing the contrast and brightness in the selected area, the Hue/Saturation tool was used to colorize the figure, rendering it a dark blue silhouette. This silhouette was copied and pasted into the photograph of the hallway.

Plain silhouette.

Silhouette enhanced with liquify and smudge tools.

Because the figure still looked a little too mundane, the layer containing the figure was selected and the Liquify tool (Image>Liquify) was used to distort its shape. Then, the Smudge tool was employed to soften and blur selected areas of the figure. Finally, the layer opacity was set to 90%.

Duplicate layer with silhouette blurred.

Flipped vertically and blurred to create shadow.

To create a shadow, the finished layer was duplicated and placed behind the original, then blurred slightly (Filter>Blur>Gaussian Blur). Its opacity was set to 50%. This new, blurred layer was flipped vertically (Edit>Transform>Flip Vertical). The Wave filter was used to distort the shape of this layer. The layer's opacity was set to 70% and it was positioned appropriately.

STEP FOUR: ADD BIRD

The top of the image still seemed a little empty, so the decision was made to add a bird in flight. A good picture of a flying bird was located, but it

Bird image.

was a seagull at the beach—not very mysterious! To make the bird fit the image, it was selected from the beach background, and then inverted (Image>Adjustments>Invert). This made the white bird black. Then, the bird was copied and pasted into the hallway image. To give the gull a greater sense of motion, the Smudge tool was used to blur the wings. Then, to add a little more interest, the Liquify tool was used to distort the body and legs slightly.

FINISHING TOUCHES

Once all of the elements were positioned correctly, the layer opacities were fine-tuned and the overall colors tweaked to make them blend as seamlessly as possible.

Final image.

AFTERWORD

Having finished reading this book and learning about the techniques covered in it, you have the knowledge to complete just about any imaging project you can dream up. This doesn't mean that you're done learning or that you'll never get frustrated (or completely puzzled). You will—*everyone* does. Photoshop is a complex program with a myriad of extremely specialized features that can take years of practice to master.

Even professionals who use Photoshop every day rarely use it (or need to know how to use it) to its full capacity. Instead, they successfully use a selection of common tools—tools used in virtually *every* digital imaging operation. You now know how to use these tools, too. All that separates you from the pros is experience.

Fortunately, gaining experience in Photoshop is a lot of fun—just find some images and put your imagination to work. You may also want to keep your eyes open for digital effects we see every day in the photos on billboards, in magazines, on television, etc.—then try to replicate the effect yourself with your own images.

As you expand your proficiency with these tools, don't be afraid to check out some of the other very specialized features and functions of Photoshop. The worst that can happen is that you make your image look terrible and have to go to Edit>Undo. Ultimately, that is the very best part of digital imaging—you can experiment to your heart's content and almost never need to start over. Good luck!

RESOURCES

▶ COLOR MANAGEMENT
Margulis, Dan. *Professional Photoshop: The Classic Guide to Color Correction, 4th ed.* (John Wiley & Sons, 2002).

▶ DIGITAL PHOTO RETOUCHING
Drafahl, Jack and Sue. *Photo Salvage with Adobe® Photoshop®* (Amherst Media, 2002).
Ferro, Rick and Deborah Lynn. *Wedding Photography with Adobe® Photoshop®* (Amherst Media, 2003).
Lute, Gwen. *Photo Retouching with Adobe® Photoshop®*, 2nd Ed. (Amherst Media, 2002).
Perkins, Michelle and Paul Grant. *Traditional Photographic Effects with Adobe® Photoshop®*, 2nd Ed. (Amherst Media, 2003).

▶ SCANNING TECHNIQUES
Sheppard, Rob. *Basic Scanning Guide for Photographers and Other Creative Types* (Amherst Media, 2001).

Williams, Robin and Sandee Cohen. *Non-Designer's Scan and Print Book* (Peachpit Press, 1999).

▶ DIGITAL PHOTOGRAPHY
Drafahl, Jack and Sue. *Advanced Digital Camera Techniques* (Amherst Media, 2003).
Drafahl, Jack and Sue. *Step-by-Step Digital Photography* (Amherst Media, 2003).
Eggers, Ron. *Basic Digital Photography* (Amherst Media, 1998).
Montizambert, Dave. *Professional Digital Photography* (Amherst Media, 2002).
Sheppard, Rob. *Beginner's Guide to Digital Imaging* (Amherst Media, 2002).

▶ BLACK & WHITE IMAGING WITH PHOTOSHOP
Schaub, George. *The Digital Darkroom: Black & White Techniques Using Photoshop* (Silver Pixel Press, 1999).

KEYBOARD SHORTCUTS

GENERAL SHORTCUTS	WINDOWS 98/NT	MacOS
Create new file	Ctrl + N	⌘ + N
Open file	Ctrl + O	⌘ + O
Save file	Ctrl + S	⌘ + S
Save as	Ctrl + Shift + S	⌘ + Shift + S
Save a copy	Ctrl + Alt + S	⌘ + Opt + N
Print	Ctrl + P	⌘ + P
Cut	Crtl + X	⌘ + X
Copy	Ctrl + C	⌘ + C
Paste	Ctrl + V	⌘ + V
Show/hide all palettes and toolbox	Tab	Tab
Show/hide all palettes except toolbox	Shift + Tab	Shift + Tab
Undo	Ctrl + Z	⌘ + Z
Accept crop, transform, dialogue box	Enter	Return or Enter
Cancel crop, transform, dialogue box	Esc or Ctrl + . (period)	Esc or ⌘ + . (period)
Help	F1	Help
Access Adobe Online	Click icon on toolbox	Click icon on toolbox
Draw/erase in straight lines	Shift + drag	Shift + drag
(with Eraser, Paintbrush, Pencil, Blur, Sharpen, Smudge, Dodge, or Burn tool)		
Select perfect circle/perfect square	Shift + drag	Shift + drag
(with Elliptical or Rectangular Marquee tool)		
Swap foreground/background colors	X	X
Select next brush (in brushes palette)	[	[
Select previous brush (in brushes palette)	]	]
Select all	Ctrl + A	⌘ + A
Deselect	Ctrl + D	⌘ + D
Add to selection	Shift + click and/or drag	Shift + click and/or drag
(with Marquee, Magic Wand or Lasso tool)		
Subtract from selection	Alt + click and/or drag	Opt + click and/or drag
(with Marquee, Magic Wand or Lasso tool)		
Inverse selection	Ctrl + Shift + I	⌘ + Shift + I
Nudge selection one pixel	Arrow key	Arrow Key
Fit image on screen	Ctrl + 0	⌘ + 0
Reapply last filter	Ctrl + F	⌘ + F
Create new layer	Ctrl + Shift + N	⌘ + Shift + N
Open Levels dialogue box	Ctrl + L	⌘ + L
Open Auto Levels dialogue box	Ctrl + Shift + L	⌘ + Shift + L
Open Curves dialogue box	Ctrl + M	⌘ + M
Open Color Balance dialogue box	Ctrl + B	⌘ + B
Open Hue/Saturation dialogue box	Ctrl + U	⌘ + U
Invert	Ctrl + I	⌘ + I

INDEX

Other Books from
Amherst Media®

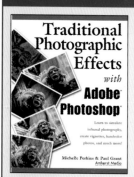

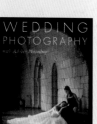

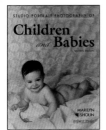

Studio Portrait Photography of Children and Babies, *2nd Edition*

Marilyn Sholin

Work with the youngest portrait clients to create cherished images. Includes tips for working with kids at every developmental stage, from infant to pre-schooler. Features: lighting, posing and much more! $29.95 list, 8½x11, 128p, 90 full-color photos, order no. 1657.

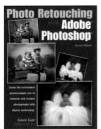

Photo Retouching with Adobe® Photoshop® *2nd Edition*

Gwen Lute

Designed for photographers, this manual teaches every phase of the process, from scanning to final output. Learn to restore damaged photos, correct imperfections, create realistic composite images and correct for dazzling color. $29.95 list, 8½x11, 120p, 60+ photos, order no. 1660.

Infrared Wedding Photography

Patrick Rice, Barbara Rice & Travis Hill

Step-by-step techniques for adding the dreamy look of black & white infrared to your wedding portraiture. Capture the fantasy of the wedding with unique ethereal portraits your clients will love! $29.95 list, 8½x11, 128p, 60 images, order no. 1681.

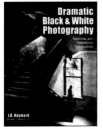

Dramatic Black & White Photography
SHOOTING AND DARKROOM TECHNIQUES

J. D. Hayward

Create dramatic fine-art images and portraits with the master b&w techniques in this book. From outstanding lighting techniques to top-notch, creative darkroom work, this book takes b&w to the next level! $29.95 list, 8½x11, 128p, order no. 1687.

Posing and Lighting Techniques for Studio Photographers

J. J. Allen

Master the skills you need to create beautiful lighting for portraits of any subject. Posing techniques for flattering, classic images help turn every portrait into a work of art. $29.95 list, 8½x11, 120p, 125 full-color photos, order no. 1697.

Studio Portrait Photography in Black & White

David Derex

From concept to presentation, you'll learn to select clothes, create beautiful lighting, and prop and pose top-quality black & white portraits in the studio. $29.95 list, 8½x11, 128p, 70 photos, order no. 1689.

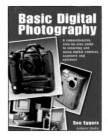

Basic Digital Photography

Ron Eggers

Step-by-step text and clear explanations teach you how to select and use all types of digital cameras. Learn all the basics with no-nonsense, easy to follow text designed to bring even true novices up to speed quickly and easily. $17.95 list, 8½x11, 80p, 40 b&w photos, order no. 1701.

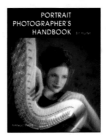

Portrait Photographer's Handbook

Bill Hurter

Bill Hurter has compiled a step-by-step guide to portraiture that easily leads the reader through all phases of portrait photography. This book will be an asset to experienced photographers and beginners alike. $29.95 list, 8½x11, 128p, full color, 60 photos, order no. 1708.

Basic Scanning Guide For Photographers and Other Creative Types

Rob Sheppard

This how-to manual is an easy-to-read, hands on workbook that offers practical knowledge of scanning. It also includes excellent sections on the mechanics of scanning and scanner selection. $17.95 list, 8½x11, 96p, 80 photos, order no. 1702.

The Art of Color Infrared Photography

Steven H. Begleiter

Color infrared photography will open the doors to an entirely new and exciting photographic world. This exhaustive book shows readers how to previsualize the scene and get the results they want. $29.95 list, 8½x11, 128p, 80 full-color photos, order no. 1728.

High Impact Portrait Photography

Lori Brystan

Learn how to create the high-end, fashion-inspired portraits your clients will love. Features posing, alternative processing and much more. $29.95 list, 8½x11, 128p, 60 full-color photos, order no. 1725.

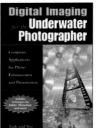

Digital Imaging for the Underwater Photographer

Jack and Sue Drafahl

This book will teach readers how to improve their underwater images with digital imaging techniques. This book covers all the bases—from color balancing your monitor, to scanning, to output and storage. $39.95 list, 6x9, 224p, 80 color photos, order no. 1727.

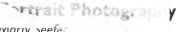

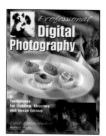
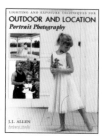
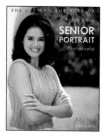
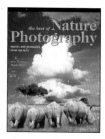
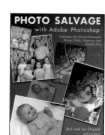